Signature
WINES & WINERIES
OF WASHINGTON

Hedges Family Estate, page 165

Noteworthy Wines From
Leading Estate and Boutique Wineries

Published by

Intermedia Publishing Services, Inc
5815 Richwater Drive
Dallas, TX 75232
972-898-8915
www.panache.com

Publisher: Brian G. Carabet
Regional Publisher: Marc Zurba
Managing Editor: Megan Winkler
Editor: Katrina Autem
Editor: Rachel Watkins
Managing Photographer: Richard Duval
Contributing Photographer: Steve Lenz
Art Director: Adam Carabet
Administrative Coordinator: Vicki Martin

Printed in Malaysia

Distributed by Independent Publishers Group
800.888.4741

PUBLISHER'S DATA

SIGNATURE WINES & WINERIES OF WASHINGTON

Library of Congress Control Number: 2016912485

ISBN: 978-0-9969653-6-1

First Printing 2018

10 9 8 7 6 5 4 3 2 1

Signature
WINES & WINERIES
OF WASHINGTON

Noteworthy Wines From Leading Estate and Boutique Wineries

Fielding Hills Winery, page 155

WASHINGTON STATE WINE

WESTERN WASHINGTON

CANADA

Bellingham

Port Angeles

LAKE CHELAN

COLUMBIA VALLEY

Woodinville

Wenatchee

Seattle

OLYMPICS

ANCIENT LAKES

47°

Olympia

PUGET SOUND

NACHES HEIGHTS

WAHLUKE SLOPE

Yakima

SNIPES MOUNTAIN

RATTLESNAKE HILLS

RED MOUNTAIN

Prosser

Tri-Cities

YAKIMA VALLEY

46°

Walla Walla

HORSE HEAVEN HILLS

COLUMBIA GORGE

Vancouver

Portland

PACIFIC OCEAN

CASCADES

©2016   www.washingtonwine.org

MI   20   40   60

20   40   60   KM

INTRODUCTION

By The Washington State Wine Commission

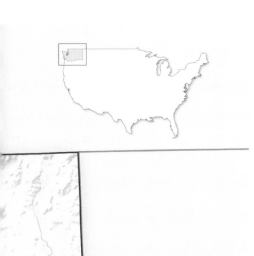

Welcome to Washington State, one of the world's most exciting and dynamic wine regions. With 14 unique growing regions, more than 900 wineries, upwards of 55,000 acres of wine grapes and growing international acclaim, Washington continues to explode onto the world stage. Signature Wines & Wineries of Washington offers an insider's look at the state's wine industry through the lens of the people and wineries that make it so special.

The Washington State wine story begins with our ancient volcanic history, and alluvial top soils deposited by a series of floods some 15,000 years ago. These top soils and the basalt-based foundation are ideally suited for wine grapes. The towering Cascade Mountain Range splits the state from evergreen coasts and snow-capped mountains to the west, to a vast sagebrush desert to the east. It is this warmer climate in Eastern Washington that provides near-perfect growing conditions for close to 70 grape varieties, primarily Cabernet Sauvignon, Merlot, Chardonnay, Riesling, and Syrah. Although wine country boasts 300 days of sunshine and plenty of heat to ripen grapes, temperatures throughout the arid region shift dramatically from day to night, preserving a beautiful natural acidity. This allows our winemakers to combine the vibrant fruit character expected of American wine with the defined structure typical of the Old World.

Modern-day winegrowing began in the 1960s, when Washington's innovative growers and winemakers broke ground in a vast, wild territory where conventional wisdom said they could not. Today's Washington winemakers carry on that mindset, refusing to be bound by convention–to push boundaries, experiment, and continuously learn along the way. A hallmark trait of the Washington State wine industry has always been an unbreakable camaraderie, as the groundbreakers knew they had to work together to build the industry as a whole. That sense of community still runs deep, as the current-day winemakers and grape growers live and work in small towns, are active in their communities, connected to the land and eager to share their stories with visitors. Together, they embrace a youthful underdog status to share their wines and message with a common vision.

From humble beginnings, Washington State wine has grown to a respected and influential industry with a $5 billion-plus economic impact to the state. Ranking second nationally for premium wine production, Washington wine is available in all 50 states and more than 100 countries. Wineries are opening at a staggering rate, doubling in the past decade to more than 900 in 2017. The land is attracting outside investors and developers, with new vineyards being planted at a breakneck pace.

In the midst of such explosive growth, Washington State wine leaders have an eye on the future. In 2003, the Washington Wine Institute and its educational partners celebrated the state's $2.3 million investment to create new two-year and four-year degree programs supporting the state's growing wine industry. A degree program, ongoing education, and research enhance the state's reputation as a quality wine-producing region. In 2011, the industry voted to increase their annual assessments to help fund a world-class Wine Science Center at Washington State University. At the completion of its construction in June 2015, the $23 million facility was the most technologically advanced wine science center in the world.

It's an exciting time to enjoy the captivating, irresistible wines of Washington State—and the best is still yet to come. Cheers!

Mercer Estates Winery, page 183

WESTERN WASHINGTON

CENTRAL WASHINGTON

Tertulia Cellars, page 305

Basel Cellars Estate Winery, page 229

WALLA WALLA VALLEY

CONTENTS

Long Shadows Vintners, page 277

Columbia Winery, page 35

WESTERN WASHINGTON

Pomum Cellars, page 49

Brian Carter Cellars, page 23

Chateau St Michelle, page 31

Seattle, Washington, is simply iconic. Unrivaled beauty, a thriving arts and culture scene, and of course, exceptional wineries make Seattle a must-see hub of activity throughout the year. The SoDo Urban Works tasting center, in particular, offers a number of wineries within walking distance of one another. Walk, ride your bike, or ride share through the neighborhood and explore the funky, sometimes irreverent, wineries that call Seattle home. In the Georgetown neighborhood, old brick buildings have been repurposed into wineries, intriguing bars, and delicious restaurants.

Dozens of wineries in Seattle make it easy to sample, compare, and pick your favorite wines from scores of options. But just 30 minutes from the city sits Woodinville, where more than 100 wineries and tasting rooms from wineries across the state await. The area's oldest winery, Chateau Ste. Michelle, imparts Old World style to the region and stands as an homage to the industry's pioneering beginnings. It is joined by other remarkable wineries that call Woodinville home.

Located in the Puget Sound AVA, the region boasts a temperate, maritime climate, making it the coolest and wettest growing region in the state. Pinot Noir is the region's most planted variety, followed by Riesling, but it's suitable to interesting varietals seen nowhere else in Washington: Regen, Siegerrebe, Madeleine Angevine, Muller Thurgau, and more.

Whether you wish to explore the bustling urban environment in Seattle, step out among the rolling hills of Woodinville, or better yet, explore both, there are more things to see and do in both areas than a day allows.

ADAMS BENCH WINERY WOODINVILLE

Driving up to Adams Bench Winery, one is immediately struck by the sense it is unlike any other. The pastoral setting about 20 miles northeast of downtown Seattle looks like the pages of a beloved collection of fairytales. Crisp white fences cut through gently rolling hills, majestic elms soar overhead, and a weathervane gently moves with the breeze atop the winery's main building.

Here, with views west toward the Olympic Mountains, Owner-Winemakers Tim and Erica Blue live their passion for wine. Tim, a Seattle trial lawyer and Erica, OB/GYN and Medical Director, developed a deep appreciation for wine and wine travel after many trips to Northern California, Oregon, Eastern Washington, and later France, Italy, and beyond. That blossomed into a second career on the 3.27-acre property where they live on Hollywood Hill in Woodinville, as well as the establishment of Adams Bench Winery and its first harvest in 2005.

FACING PAGE: Flowers in bloom in the gardens and beautiful landscaping greets visitors as they approach the winery.

TOP LEFT: A relaxed pastural setting makes for a relaxing day tasting wine at Adams Bench Winery.

TOP RIGHT: Erica Blue inspects the crop in the vineyard during harvest.
Photographs courtesy of Adams Bench Winery

In the winery's first public event two years later, the barrel tastings led to a pre-release sold-out 2005 vintage. It was clear the Blues knew how to make exceptional wine, and the critics quickly agreed. In October 2009, Robert Parker's Wine Advocate hailed Adams Bench Winery a "Rising Star" on the Washington wine scene, and rated their 2006 wines 93, 91. Since then, Adams Bench wines have been consistently rated 90-plus points in Wine Advocate,

Wine Spectator, Wine Enthusiast, and in other local and national reviews. There's a waiting list for Membership in the winery's Collectors Club.

Adams Bench produces 1,000 cases a year of Cabernet Sauvignon and Cabernet blends, routinely makes Sangiovese, ,and occasionally other single varietal wines from fruit typically reserved for blending, all reds, no whites. Daughter Hannah Lewis works with the Blues as Assistant Winemaker.

Each year Collectors Club Members and guests look forward to the latest vintage of the winery's flagship wines, Columbia Valley Cabernet Sauvignon "the V" and Columbia Valley "Reckoning,"- served multiple times at the concluding dinner of the Microsoft CEO Summit, the annual gathering in Seattle of world leaders and Fortune 500 CEOs-along with an impressive lineup of single vineyard Cabernets.

LEFT: Late summer hot air balloon over Hollywood Hill, Adams Bench Winery.
Photograph courtesy of Adams Bench Winery

ABOVE: Looking west over the winery courtyard toward the Olympic Mountains during harvest season.
Photograph by Sheri Solvang Nohle

BELOW: Winery dogs Freddy and Grace in the Winery tasting room.
Photograph by Julie Austin

COLUMBIA VALLEY CABERNET SAUVIGNON
"the V"

GOURMET PAIRINGS

Pairs perfectly with fire-grilled filet mignon, medium rare, served with creamy mashed potatoes and slightly charred asparagus stalks.

TASTING NOTES

The word "Vibrance" ("the V") expresses what the winemakers relish in a well-made Cabernet Sauvignon, a wine fully alive, the product of carefully managed fruit, harvested at ripeness, yielding tiny berries with intense flavor and color, undiminished by the winemaking approach. This wine opens with sensuous aromas of black currant, violet, and cassis, with an elegant mouthfeel of sequential notes of caramel, black cherry, pencil lead, smoke, and a long lingering finish. Though Adams Bench produces a lineup of impressive single vineyard Cabernets for its fully-subscribed Collectors Club, "the V" is a favorite of the winemakers and serves as the winery's flagship Cabernet.

WINEMAKER'S INSIGHT

Fruit grown to low tonnage per acre and hand-harvested at ripeness enters the winemaking process that is directed at emphasizing skin tannins while avoiding seed tannins. Destemmed grapes are fermented as whole berries, without crushing, in open-top stainless-steel tanks with twice-daily punch downs during fermentation. Pressing to taste when dry, using an upright stainless basket press, the wine undergoes malolactic fermentation in the barrel, before being bottled unfined and unfiltered.

AWARDS & DISTINCTIONS

Consistently rated 90-93 points by Wine Advocate, Wine Spectator, Wine Enthusiast, and other reviewers. Top 100 Washington Wine in multiple publications for multiple years.

TECHNICAL DATA

APPELLATION: Horse Heaven Hills, Yakima Valley and Columbia Valley
COMPOSITION: 80 – 90% Cabernet Sauvignon with small quantities of Merlot, Cabernet Franc, or both
MATURATION: Aged 20-22 months in 100% new French Oak
CELLARING: This wine is age-worthy for 20-plus years

LEARN MORE

Learn more about this wine and our winery by scanning the image on the left

COLUMBIA VALLEY RECKONING

GOURMET PAIRINGS

The rich, savory flavor and texture of comforting food like handmade pasta Bolognese matches perfectly with Reckoning.

TASTING NOTES

Reckoning, as highly-rated as any at its price point, is full-bodied, balanced, well-structured, and satisfying. Aromas of red currant and raspberry open to barrel spice, bramble, cocoa, and crème brûlée coating every corner of the palate. The wine is approachable in its youth but age-worthy with sufficient backbone to pair well with a variety of foods from rustic to serious. It's another favorite of the winemakers, first produced in the winery's second year and its flagship red blend.

WINEMAKER'S INSIGHT

The winery's approach in the vineyard and cellar is virtually identical to Cabernet Sauvignon "the V" and the winery's lineup of single vineyard Cabernets and other wines: fruit is grown at low tonnage per acre, harvested at ripeness, managed to produce a wine realizing all the potential carefully tended fruit has to offer. The wine is then bottled unfined and unfiltered. Fruit from Mays Discovery Vineyard in Horse Heaven Hills, Red Willow Vineyard in Yakima Valley, and Stillwater Creek Vineyard in Frenchman Hills of the North Central Columbia Valley is used to make the Reckoning. Vines range in age from approximately 15 years to three decades.

AWARDS AND DISTINCTIONS

Consistently ranked 90+ points by Wine Advocate, Wine Spectator, Wine Enthusiast, and other local and national reviewers.

TECHNICAL DATA

APPELLATION: Horse Heaven Hills, Yakima Valley, Columbia Valley
COMPOSITION: Dominated by Cabernet Sauvignon and Merlot, with contributions from Cabernet Franc, Petit Verdot, or Malbec
MATURATION: Aged 20-22 months in 100% French Oak, 80% new
CELLARING: Released a year after bottling, age-worthy for15-20 years

LEARN MORE

Learn more about this wine and our winery by scanning the image on the left

When visitors arrive at Adams Bench Winery, they're struck by the serene landscape and charm of the winemakers themselves, who are always ready to chat about winemaking philosophy and the origin of the winery's name. Lush hydrangea, lavender, and gentle paths lead past a small Craftsman-style winery production barn adjacent to a two-story structure housing the tasting room and underground barrel cellar. An occasional hot air balloon overhead or visitor arriving on horseback for tasting adds to the serene setting.

As Adams Bench Winery continues to evolve into the next decade and beyond, it will remain a beloved destination, and the wines will surely continue to captivate wine appreciators for generations to come.

ABOVE: Looking toward the iconic chapel on the hill at Red Willow Vineyard, late in the harvest season.

RIGHT: Winemaker Tim Blue hard at work on the crush pad sampling from the barrel.
Photographs courtesy of Adams Bench Winery

BARRAGE CELLARS WOODINVILLE

Passion for winemaking and big, bold flavors meet in Barrage Cellars wines. Founding winemaker and owner Kevin Correll began his career in winemaking after taking his own advice: "If you love what you do, you'll never consider it work, and you need to make sure you're happy in your job." The advice was initially for his daughter, but Kevin then realized he wanted an early and fun retirement for himself and his wife. So, he began making wine in his garage as most hobbyists do, and volunteered at larger, established wineries to learn the ropes. It was at one of these wineries—in a facility housed in a remodeled barn—that his first barrel production and the name of his winery were born. In a play on words, garage-barn, barn-garage, and as an homage to his winemaking style, Barrage Cellars' name was a perfect fit.

Since establishing the winery in 2006, and since receiving his Enology degree from UC Davis, Kevin has crafted brilliant Bordeaux-style wines and some unique whites. Cabernet Sauvignon, Cabernet Franc, Merlot, and Syrah comprise the winery's red offerings, while an elegant Chardonnay and an aged in concrete Viognier are the extent of the winery's white wines available to the public. Wine club members enjoy small quantities of Petit Verdot, Petite Sirah, GSM—a Grenache, Syrah, and Mourvedre blend—Pinot Noir, and Malbec depending on the year. Relying on the help of volunteers to assist with production, bottling, and tasting room/events, Kevin and wife, Bonni, ultimately run the winery themselves. While Kevin creates the wines, Bonni manages the tasting room and all business aspects of the winery including distribution, accounting, and public relations, but it's their grandson Decker who's the big star.

FACING PAGE: Winemaker, Kevin Correll, tying down and readying for transport a load of Cabernet Franc grapes off of Red Willow Vineyard in the Yakima Valley AVA.

TOP LEFT: The true romantic part of winemaking is popping the cork and pouring a glass.

TOP RIGHT: We three: It's been a joy raising our grandson who's title around the winery is "Assistant Winemaker." We'll have to see if that really materializes!
Photographs by Richard Duval

DOUBLE BARREL CABERNET SAUVIGNON

GOURMET PAIRINGS

Grilled ribeye with chimichurri or Cabernet Sauvignon braised beef short ribs make perfect companions for the Double Barrel Cabernet Sauvignon.

TASTING NOTES

A classic example of Cabernet Sauvignon from the Red Mountain AVA. This wine has aromas of blackberry and red fruit with a hint of violets. It is full-bodied with lots of cherries, plums with big structure, and fine-grain tannin.

WINEMAKER'S INSIGHT

Fruit is hand-picked, hand-sorted, and fermented in one-ton, open top fermentation vats with two to three punch downs daily. The wine has much skin contact and is treated with a very soft hand to create an elegant yet robust outcome.

AWARDS AND DISTINCTIONS

Rated 90+ points with major publications and in competitions
Silver medal – 2018 San Francisco Chronicle

TECHNICAL DATA

APPELLATION: Red Mountain
COMPOSITION: 100% Cabernet Sauvignon
MATURATION: Aged 24 months in 50% once used French oak
CELLARING: This wine is great now but built to last for the next 10 to 15 years

JOIN OUR WINE CLUB

Find out more about our Wine Club by scanning the image on the left

In fact, when Decker is otherwise occupied and not at the winery, visitors familiar with Barrage Cellars are disappointed in his absence. Ask him what he owns at the winery and he'll tell you the forklift belongs to him!

Guests enjoy connecting with Kevin and Bonni personally—and Decker when they get the chance—when they visit Barrage Cellars, located in the Woodinville Warehouse District. It's open on Saturdays and Sundays, or by appointment and while there, guests can chat with Kevin about his winemaking philosophy and peek at the inner workings of the winery, including the 5,000-pound concrete egg where the Viognier is aged. You will even find Kevin offering barrel samples some days.

Ultimately, it is the exceptional wine that tempts guest back to the winery year after year. Each wine showcases the best of what its vineyard has to offer. Flavor-packed fruit from Boushey Vineyard in Yakima Valley delights on the palate as it complements or comprises the winery's single vineyard Merlot, Cabernet Franc, Chardonnay, or Viognier offerings. Fruit from Red Willow Vineyard gives structure, character, and acidity to both the Cabernet Franc and Merlot, and Red Mountain fruit from Quintessence and Shaw Vineyards make the Cabernet

Sauvignon equal to none. As most winemakers are fond of saying, you can't make high-quality wine without high-quality fruit, and Kevin swears by the sentiment.

The critics agree—Barrage Cellars wines are captivating, elegant, and highlight the region's different terroirs well. The AKA Columbia Valley Merlot is a favorite among Wine Advocate writers, receiving 90+ points for multiple vintages. The Cease and Desist Yakima Valley Cabernet Franc, crafted from fruit from Boushey and Red Willow Vineyards, wows with its drinkability, purity, and texture. It also received 90-92+ points from various publications while the Double Barrel 100 percent Red Mountain Cabernet Sauvignon has been described as "sexy and voluptuous on the palate," by Wine Advocate. Finally, Kevin's Boushey Vineyard Syrah has been touted as "almost over the top" by Jay Miller, previously of Wine Advocate.

TOP: You're more than just a customer when you visit Barrage Cellars tasting room, friendships are made around our table.
Photograph by Richard Duval

The winery has not been able to have the Viognier scored as the wine club buys it out each year, prompting Barrage Cellars to increase production to share this wine with others. The most current wines before publication were entered into the 2018 San Francisco Chronicle Wine Competition—where nearly 7,000 wines were considered—and earned Barrage Cellars prestigious medals. The 2013 Cease & Desist Cabernet earned Double Gold, the 2013 Double Barrel Cabernet Sauvignon received Silver, the 2013 Quinella Merlot received Bronze, and the 2016 Nuclear Blonde Chardonnay took home the Silver medal. Truly, the lineage of all Kevin's wines holds prestigious points and scores showing that Kevin Correll of Barrage Cellars is a hidden gem.

Wine Club members receive wines twice a year and enjoy exclusive wine release parties in spring and fall. Barrage Cellars participates in numerous functions throughout the year and offers private tours as rewards for the highest bidder. Events include the Auction of Washington Wines, the Evergreen Hospital Gala, Grapes on the Green- Benaroya Research Institute for Virginia Mason, the JDRF Gala, and events for the Children's Hospital Uncompensated Care Guilds to mention a few.

TOP: Barrage Cellars tasting room currently undergoing a remodel...Are you feeling Barn and Garage vibes yet?

RIGHT: Outside look at warehouse entry to Barrage Cellars tasting room, it's not pretty but what's inside is pretty awesome.
Photographs by Richard Duval

SECRET WEAPON SYRAH

GOURMET PAIRINGS

The ripe, elegant flavors of our Secret Weapon Syrah pair perfectly with smoked pork belly with a Syrah-reduction glaze.

TASTING NOTES

Classic Washington State black and blue fruits, pepper, and spice with hints of mint and smoke enhance the full-bodied wine. It's ripe yet still elegant, with a fresh profile on the palete. The color is inky black as you swirl, and it coats the side of your glass.

WINEMAKER'S INSIGHT

The Secret Weapon name is dedicated to my best single vineyard, single varietal lot for each vintage. The Secret Weapon has been Cabernet Franc, Cabernet Sauvignon, and Syrah to date. The decision is made right before bottling while tasting through barrels individually.

AWARDS & DISTINCTIONS

92 points – Wine Advocate

TECHNICAL DATA

APPELLATION: Varies
COMPOSITION: 100% varietal – Syrah, Cabernet Franc, or Cabernet Sauvignon
MATURATION: Aged 26 months in 100% new oak
CELLARING: Extremely approachable upon release but built to last for the next 20+ years

LEARN MORE

Learn more about this wine and our winery by scanning the image on the left

BRIAN CARTER CELLARS WOODINVILLE

Balance is key at Brian Carter Cellars, where blends take center stage, and each bottle tells a story. Owner and winemaker Brian Carter was drawn to wine at a young age, not because his parents were in the industry or enjoyed wine, but because he was given a microscope at age 12. He was intrigued by something called yeast, and he wanted to see what it looked like at a microscopic level. He was told that if he wanted to look at yeast, he would have to start a fermentation. So he picked some blackberries, made wine, took a sample, and was delighted at what he saw. Since then, Brian has been making that yeast work for him as he blends exceptionally balanced wines that captivate the palate.

Since arriving on the Washington wine scene in 1980—when there were just 16 wineries open—Brian has crafted a career centered on his love of the science behind winemaking and the art of creating an experience through wine. He studied microbiology at Oregon State University and developed an appreciation for Oregon's wines while there. After two years at UC Davis, in the School of Enology, and experience at landmark California wineries including Mount Eden Vineyard and Chateau Montelena, Brian had honed his winemaking skill. Drawn to the vineyards and wineries of Washington, Brian joined Paul Thomas Winery and enjoyed noteworthy success as a young winemaker, including beating Chateaux Lafite Rothchild at a tasting in New York City with his 1983 Cabernet Sauvignon.

Over the years, Brian consulted for a series of emerging wineries and in 1997 began producing his own wine, Solesce, at the Apex Winery, where he was

the resident winemaker and co-owner. The wine sold out quickly, and it became apparent that it was time for Brian to establish his own winery. In 2004, he started Brian Carter Cellars, and released the full line of Brian Carter Wines in 2006, the same year the winery's tasting room opened in Woodinville. Located in a charming old home in a prominent location in Woodinville's Hollywood area, the tasting room offers guests the chance to sample selections while relaxing on the deck and enjoying views of the Sammamish River agricultural area and Mt. Rainier. Wine Club members are able to enjoy a private tasting room offering member exclusive wine selections.

Each year, Brian and fellow winemaker, Robert Takahashi, bring in up to 20 different varietals to craft 10 or more different wines, offering something for just about any taste. Abracadabra is an enchanting red blend whose "magic" comes from a different varietal mix each year, depending on the characteristics of the vintage's harvest. Blended from traditional red grape varieties, it's anything but traditional.

TOP LEFT: All of Brian Carter's grapes are hand-picked, hand-sorted, and punched down by hand.
Photograph by Carol Hook

BELOW LEFT: Todd Newhouse and Brian Carter inspecting Tempranillo grapes while pondering how they can make these great grapes even greater.
Photograph by Richard Duvall.

ABOVE: Brian Carter walking amongst the vines to determine the timing of harvesting this year's crop.
Photograph by Richard Duvall

FACING PAGE; Our Oriana pairs well with scallops like these expertly prepared by Tandem Wine Bar in Woodinville.
Photograph by Richard Duvall

ORIANA

GOURMET PAIRINGS

The wine's complexity, and refreshing balance, makes it a great match for an array of dishes from chicken to shellfish. Brian's favorite is crab cakes with fruit-based salsa, or step up the volume by matching it with Cajun spiced prawns.

TASTING NOTES

Hardly a month goes by without someone telling the winery that Oriana is their favorite white wine. With its seductive aromas and perfect balance, its popularity just keeps soaring. The wine is richly aromatic, resplendent with tangerine, apricot, ripe pear, and apple, with touches of honey and anise. Crisp acidity greets the palate while mouth-filling fruit flavors linger.

WINEMAKER'S INSIGHT

The grapes are hand-picked and whole cluster pressed grapes; 30 percent barrel fermented in neutral barrels with sur lie and bâttonage. The wine is blended and bottled in the spring, six months after the vintage.

AWARDS AND DISTINCTIONS

Multiple awards including Gold Medals at Seattle Wine Awards
90+ scores – Wine Enthusiast and Wine Advocate

TECHNICAL DATA

APPELLATION: Yakima Valley
COMPOSITION: Dominated by Viognier and Roussanne, with an addition of 10 to 15% Riesling.
MATURATION: Aged six months in a combination of neutral barrels and stainless steel.
CELLARING: Best enjoyed within three to four years of the vintage

LEARN MORE

Buy Oriana in our store by scanning image on left or visit https://www.briancartercellars.com

BYZANCE

GOURMET PAIRINGS

Great balance and a hint of tannin make this wine a great match for a wide range of food, especially medium bodied or braised meats such as chicken, veal, and pork. Brian's personal favorite pairing is with medium-rare duck breast, served on a bed of risotto and finished with red wine demi-glace.

TASTING NOTES

With a complex nose of bright red cherries, tar, white pepper, and the garrigue spice that you get walking the fields of Provence, this wine explodes in your mouth with lots of bright fruit and finishes with a long, slightly earthy and mineral notes.

WINEMAKER'S INSIGHT

European-style blended wines are my passion. No wine, no region inspires Brian more than Chateauneuf de Pape, and the terroir in Washington is expressing itself with an identity truly reminiscent of the Southern Rhone. Today the flavors we are getting out of the Grenache with its ripe cherry character has even surpassed the greatness of Washington Syrah. The incredibly important addition of Mourvedre with its spice and structure, and more recently the high notes of Counoise and Cinsault add complexity and depth. Grapes are hand-picked, hand-sorted, and punched down by hand in small fermenters, 50 percent whole cluster Grenache and Syrah, with minimal racking to preserve fruit. Extra time in the barrel and bottle develop robust aromatics.

AWARDS AND DISTINCTIONS

Best of Show at Tri-Cities Wine Festival
Gold and Double Gold – Seattle Wine Awards
Multiple 90+ scores – Wine Advocate and Wine Enthusiast

TECHNICAL DATA

APPELLATION: Columbia Valley
COMPOSITION: Dominated by Grenache, blended with Syrah and Mourvedre; smaller amounts of Counoise and Cinsault are also added.
MATURATION: Aged 22 months in 500-liter French and European puncheons
CELLARING: Delicious now and for 10 to 14 years into the future

LEARN MORE

Learn more about Brian Carter Cellars by scanning the image on the left or visit www.briancartercellars.com

LEFT: Bysance with a perfect food pairing at Tandem Wine Bar.
Photograph by Richard Duvall

TOP: Guests enjoy wine, gifts and a welcoming ambience at our Woodinville tasting room.
Photograph by Carol Hook

BELOW: Guests toasting Brian Carter's newest release at our Woodinville tasting room.
Photograph by Carol Hook

Also in the portfolio is the Abracadabra Rosé, an equally magical blend featuring aromas of ripe strawberries and subtle notes of peaches and orange blossoms. Latin for "golden lady," Oriana is a white blend of primarily white Rhône varieties that boasts crisp acidity and a rich aroma of tangerine, apricot, ripe pear, and apple with touches of honey and anise. Tuttorosso—Italian for "all red"—is a Sangiovese based blend inspired by the super-Tuscan wines of Italy and brings to mind the richness of Tuscany in autumn. A southern Rhône-style blend, Byzance, French for "luxurious," is just that: a luscious red blend with a complex nose of bright red cherries, tar, white pepper, and garrigue spice reminiscent of the fields of Provence.

Rounding out the portfolio are: Corrida, a Tempranillo-based Rioja-style blend with a garnet hue and a lingering finish; Le Coursier, a right bank-inspired Bordeaux blend with generous aromas and an age-worthy balance; Trentenaire, a unique Petit Verdot-based blend; and Solesce, the left bank or Cabernet Sauvignon-dominated blend that started it all. Brian and his team regularly create other blends depending on the grape varieties acquired, leaving consumers continually thirsty for the magic produced each year at Brian Carter Cellars.

CALLAN CELLARS

Never in Lisa Callan's wildest dreams did she think she would own a winery. When she went back to school in 2010, enrolling in Washington State University's Enology program, it was simply to follow a hobby and learn as much about the winemaking process as she could. Along the way, she completely fell in love with it. All of it.

Not only was Lisa fascinated by the sheer amount of science in winemaking, the artistic creativity, passion, and hard work behind every bottle captivated her. So, she quickly went from making wine in her garage with help from friends, to working for other wineries and eventually acting as assistant winemaker. She gained valuable hands-on experience and skill, which proved very helpful when establishing Callan Cellars in 2015 with husband, Michael—a decision made after much thought and a family meeting in the hot tub, which Lisa firmly supports as the "best place to have a legit meeting!"

It turned out to be an inspired decision. Callan Cellars' current production facility and tasting room debuted in 2017, and the first vintage of white wines included the award-winning Picpoul and Grenache Blanc from Boushey Vineyards. Lisa loves the bright, citrusy, and acidic notes from these Rhône varietals. Her reds are just as special, too. The Cabernet Sauvignon and Syrah are made from grapes sourced from vineyards including Red Mountains Quintessence and Ciel du Cheval as well as Boushey and Dineen in the Yakima Valley. The micro-boutique winery has already developed a reputation for wonderfully offbeat Rhône-style white wines and delicious reds from Washington's most notable vineyards. Not bad for this wild dream come true.

FACING PAGE: Owner Lisa Callan proudly shares one of their latest wines in the barrel room at Callan Cellars.
Photograph by Bobby May

TOP LEFT: Mike and Lisa Callan in the Callan Cellars tasting room in Woodinville.
Photograph by Delaney Callan

TOP RIGHT: The Callan Cellars' Syrah vineyard in Ciel du Cheval.
Photograph by Delaney Callan

CHATEAU STE. MICHELLE WOODINVILLE

Like many early Washington winemakers, the founders of Chateau Ste. Michelle were inspired to prove that exceptional wines didn't have to come from California or Europe alone. They based their aspirations on the early research conducted by Dr. Walter Clore of Washington State University, which showed that Eastern Washington's growing conditions and soil were ideal for wine grapes. Sure enough, they were right to follow their instincts and thus helped establish a culture of ongoing research, community development, and the cultivation of the region's wine industry. Founded in 1934, the winery pioneered vinifera grape growing in the state and has been producing classic European varietal wines under the Ste. Michelle label since 1967. Now under the direction of Ted Baseler, President and CEO, Chateau Ste. Michelle boasts 3,900 acres of vineyards in the Columbia Valley of Eastern Washington, including the Canoe Ridge Estate and Cold Creek, LIVE and Salmon Safe-Certified vineyards.

Bob Bertheau, Senior Director of Winemaking, heads the winemaking process with the help of Red Winemaker Ray McKee and White Winemaker David Rosenthal. Together, they craft an extensive portfolio of wines that has earned the winery a vast collection of awards including 22 Top 100 Wineries of the Year honors from Wine & Spirits and 18 Top 100 Wines designations from Wine Spectator. As one of the longest-running wineries in the state, Chateau Ste. Michelle is not only noted for its award-winning, yet approachable wines, but also its long history of community involvement.

FACING PAGE: The entrance to Chateau Ste. Michelle winery, located in Woodinville, Washington. More than 300,000 guests visit Chateau Ste. Michelle winery each year.
Photograph by J.D. Smith

ABOVE: Chateau Ste. Michelle's "chateau" opened in 1976 for winemaking and visitor tours in Woodinville.
Photograph by Kevin Cruff

COLD CREEK VINEYARD
CABERNET SAUVIGNON

GOURMET PAIRINGS
Our Cold Creek Vineyard Cabernet Sauvignon pairs well with a delicious beef tenderloin steak, hearty pasta dishes, or veal.

TASTING NOTES
Cabernet Sauvignon from this iconic 45-year-old vineyard consistently delivers power, structure, and rich, concentrated black fruit. The wine offers black cherry flavors and chocolate notes with typical Cold Creek density and palate-friendly power.

WINEMAKER'S INSIGHT
Planted in 1973, the south-facing Cold Creek Vineyard is a warm, dry site with high heat accumulation, producing small clusters and small berries for intense varietal flavors and deep color. After a cutting-edge receiving and destemming system, the fruit receives daily gentle pumpovers to extract optimal flavor and color, while minimizing harsh tannins. Frequent airative racking during barrel aging softens tannins and enhances mouthfeel. Prolonged malolactic fermentation in barrels provides better complexity and integration.

AWARDS AND DISTINCTIONS
Thirty-four 90-plus scores across the industry
Wine Spectator Top 100 Wine

TECHNICAL DATA

APPELLATION: Columbia Valley
COMPOSITION: 100% Cold Creek Vineyard Cabernet Sauvignon
MATURATION: Aged approximately 21 months in a combination of new American and French Oak
CELLARING: Delicious upon release and maintains vibrancy and life well into its 20s and 30s

ORDER THIS WINE

Enter our store by scanning image on left, or visit www.ste-michelle.com/our-wines

The net proceeds of its annual Summer Concert Series help fund its charitable giving program, which supports some 400 non-profit organizations, and the winery hosts several events throughout the year. In 2002, the winery established a scholarship program that supports high-achieving, underrepresented minority undergraduates at Washington universities, as well as the Viticulture and Enology Program at Washington State University.

Located just 15 miles from Seattle, Chateau Ste. Michelle transports visitors to a place that feels as if they're strolling the historic grounds of a European estate. In 2017, the winery's French-style chateau tasting room was given a major renovation in celebration of the winery's 50th year. At 22,731 square feet, the renovated site is double the size of the previous tasting room, and includes an 80-seat theater, interactive blending room, private tasting salons, and a club lounge. There's so much to do, in fact, that guests often find themselves joyfully losing track of time during their visit.

LEFT: The newly renovated Visitor Center offers innovative wine & culinary experiences for visitors.
Photograph by Kevin Cruff

TOP : Between its winery tours, summer concert series and culinary classes, Chateau Ste. Michelle is a major tourist destination in the Seattle area.
Photograph courtesy of Chateau Ste. Michelle

BOTTOM: The Summer Concert Series was launched in 1984 and has featured top artists including Stevie Wonder, Bob Dylan, Paul Simon, John Legend, Harry Connick Jr., and more.
Photograph by Kevin Cruff

COLUMBIA WINERY   WOODINVILLE

In 1962, a relentlessly curious group of friends sought to prove the world-class quality of Washington wines, establishing what would become Columbia Winery. This ambitious assembly of 10 friends—including six University of Washington professors—aspired to honor the exceptional growing regions of the Columbia Valley. Nestled in the shadow of the majestic Olympic and Cascade Mountains, low rainfall and long days of intense sunlight create a unique climate capable of producing an array of diverse grape varieties. The history and terroir of the Columbia Valley are found in every sip of the winery's four, nationally available wines: Chardonnay, Cabernet Sauvignon, Merlot and Red Blend. The Columbia Winery tasting room, located in the heart of Woodinville wine country, offers small-lot wines sourced from renowned sites such as Red Mountain, Horse Heaven Hills, Wahluke Slope, Yakima Valley and Ancient Lakes.

For many years, Master of Wine, David Lake, maintained the founders' curious spirit and solidified their status as an iconic Washington winery. With his guidance, Columbia Winery produced the state's first series of vineyard-designated wines. He was also the first to plant several new grape varieties in the state, including Syrah, Pinot Gris and Cabernet Franc. These varieties are still vital to the region, especially Syrah, which has earned a multitude of critical acclaim.

The current team, led by Winemaker, Sean Hails, continues the tradition of crafting exceptional wines with a passion for creating a memorable experience. They continue to source fruit from a wide range of Washington's premier

FACING PAGE: Columbia Winery flags welcome visitors to the tasting room, located in the heart of Woodinville wine country.

ABOVE: Columbia Winery's grand Modern-Victorian tasting room is a sight to behold. Events are held here all throughout the year as well as daily wine tastings.
Photographs by Colleen Cahill Studios

American Viticultural Areas (AVAs). With each vintage, Hails and team select each vineyard site, refining the winery's oak program and cellar techniques to gift the wines with nuance, texture and complexity that enthusiasts and critics have come to appreciate.

As guests travel to the historic Woodinville tasting room, they're immediately struck by the spectacular, Modern-Victorian building. White wood paneling, decorative shingles and handsome black trim make up the façade. Vaulted eaves, eye-catching balconies, and rows of shining window panes bring the stately building together. The inviting outdoors and the friendly team within welcome visitors into the elegant tasting room. Striking copper pieces are woven throughout the space, melding with natural wood and concrete elements.

Certified Sommelier and Wine Educator, Shelly Fitzgerald hosts educational tastings and offers captivating insights on the Washington State wine industry. She also teaches a variety of classes for anyone curious to learn more, regardless of their level of wine knowledge. From the "Wine Foundations" class, which highlights major growing regions and important grape varietals to "Exploring What's in the Glass," where you learn how to evaluate wine like a sommelier, the experiences are fun and fulfilling.

TOP: When the sun is shining, there is no better place to bask in its warmth than Columbia Winery's outdoor plaza.

ABOVE: Columbia's forward-thinking philosophy continues in the hands of the talented and creative winemaking team, led by Winemaker Sean Hails. *Photographs by Colleen Cahill Studios*

In addition to the four nationally available varietals, the winery also offers Barbera, Merlot, Malbec, Tempranillo, Viognier, Rosé and Riesling at the tasting room and online. Visitors can enhance their tasting room experience with a selection of Northwest-inspired culinary offerings.

Columbia Winery hosts events for Wine Club members and the public throughout the year, such as Friday Night Live music, Wine Club Mixers, and the Barrel Experience where attendees can taste a sneak peek of future wines. The tasting room also has spacious event areas, perfect for large corporate events and simply magical for weddings. Furthermore, as one of the founding wineries in Washington State, Columbia Winery believes in giving back. The winery works with organizations including Seattle Children's Hospital and the Oregon Food Bank to drive their continued mission of supporting their local community.

No matter how you choose to experience Columbia Winery, there is one thing that's certain: it will be unlike any other.

TOP: Guests of Columbia Winery are invited to experience intimate wine tastings, interactive educational opportunities and sample the inventive Northwest-inspired pairings crafted by the culinary team.
Photograph by Ari Rollnick, Kabookaboo

ABOVE: Columbia's Certified Sommelier and Wine Educator, Shelly Fitzgerald hosts educational tastings for anyone curious to learn more, regardless of their level of wine knowledge.
Photograph by Colleen Cahill Studios

COLUMBIA WINERY VISION RED BLEND

GOURMET PAIRINGS

Versatile and remarkably food-friendly, Columbia Winery Vision Red Blend pairs well with savory meats such as lamb sliders with Greek mint yogurt and cucumbers, fresh spinach, and grilled onions.

TASTING NOTES

Winemaker, Sean Hails had the vision to create a distinctive Red Blend that stood apart because of its color, flavor, and finish. Keeping with his goal of crafting a Rhone-style blend, he brought together three classic Rhone grape varieties: Syrah, Grenache, and Mourvèdre. The nose is filled with aromas of delicious ripe Bing cherries and cranberries and has a unique pepper spice note from the Mourvèdre. On the palate, red fruits, plum and cherry pie filling combine with soft tannins for a long, smooth finish.

WINEMAKER'S INSIGHT

Columbia Valley features volcanic, well-drained, sandy loam soils that stress the vines to yield focused flavors in our grapes. After harvest, grapes were destemmed at the winery and transferred to tanks. We performed a saignee method on a portion of the Grenache to enhance color and structure. Fermentation occurred at around 85 degrees Fahrenheit in small-lot, stainless-steel tanks. During fermentation, pump-overs were used for intense extraction of color and flavor. Malolactic fermentation was completed to create a rounder mouthfeel.

AWARDS AND DISTINCTIONS

91 points – JebDunnuck.com

TECHNICAL DATA

APPELLATION: Columbia Valley
COMPOSITION: 90% Cabernet Sauvignon, 3% Syrah, 3% Malbec, 2% Merlot, 2% Cabernet Franc
MATURATION: Aged 18 months in 100% new French Bordeaux puncheons
CELLARING: Enjoy upon release and for decades to come

LEARN MORE

Visit our website by scanning the image on the left or or go to www.ColumbiaWinery.com

RED MOUNTAIN CABERNET SAUVIGNON

GOURMET PAIRINGS

Beautifully structured with firm tannins, Columbia Winery Red Mountain Cabernet Sauvignon pairs wonderfully with pan-seared Northwest salmon and morel mushrooms.

TASTING NOTES

Columbia Winery Red Mountain Cabernet Sauvignon opens with elegant aromas of brambleberry and a hint of blueberry. On the palate, big, bold flavors of blackberry and dark cherry meld seamlessly with toasted oak, vanilla, and spice. This wine is well-structured with firm tannins and a smooth, lingering finish.

WINEMAKER'S INSIGHT

The Red Mountain AVA produces some of the state's most intensely flavorful Cabernet Sauvignon. The vineyard site we have selected for this wine is on the western end of the mountain, with a perfect southern aspect. After harvesting, the grapes were destemmed at the winery and transferred to tanks. Fermentation occurred at 85 degrees to 90 degrees Fahrenheit in small-lot, stainless-steel tanks after a couple of days of cold soak on the skins. During fermentation, pump overs and rack and returns were used for intense extraction of color and flavor. Malolactic fermentation was completed to soften the acid level and create a complex mouthfeel.

AWARDS & DISTINCTIONS

90 points – Wine Spectator

TECHNICAL DATA

APPELLATION: Red Mountain

COMPOSITION: Predominantly Cabernet Sauvignon with additional amounts of Malbec, Cabernet Franc and Petit Verdot; percentages depend on vintage

MATURATION: Aged 18 months in combination with new and used French and American oak, 50% new

CELLARING: Beautiful now, but can be cellared up to 15 years

ORDER OUR WINE

Shop our wine store by scanning the image to left or visit www.ColumbiaWinery.com

DAMSEL CELLARS WOODINVILLE

Not all damsels are in distress—especially not Damsel Cellars winemaker-owner Mari Womack. She's more like the heroine of this story, what with her wines that are at once sophisticated and playful, elegant and powerful. Naturally, there is plenty of romance bottled up in her wines, too—befitting of the winery's fairytale-inspired name.

Mari's love affair with wine began early on when she worked in Seattle restaurants during college. The pure art of food and wine pairings—and how the right combinations could be nothing short of magical—captured not only her curiosity, but also her heart and her imagination. However, it wasn't until 2010, when she began working in Woodinville tasting rooms and volunteering at Baer Winery during harvest, that she really started delving into the world of winemaking.

Becoming a part of the Woodinville wine community fostered Mari's enthusiasm for every aspect winemaking—from grape to glass—and encouraged her to dream big and boldly. She became the assistant winemaker at Darby Winery in 2011, in effect making a deal with winemaker-owner Darby English to manage his tasting rooms if he would teach her how to make wine. Turns out, it was a pretty good deal.

LEFT Overlooking rows of Cabernet Sauvignon at Stillwater Creek Vineyard.
Photograph by Mari Womack

ABOVE: Mari in the winery among her barrels.
Photograph by Sara Womack

Mari started making wine under her own Damsel Cellars label in 2012, sourcing grapes from premium vineyards including Stillwater Creek and Boushey Vineyards. She has a special passion for Rhône varietals and single-vineyard wines with a portfolio that includes Syrah, Grenache, Mourvedre, Cabernet

Sauvignon, Cabernet Franc, and Malbec. She likes to emulate the delicacy and restraint in Old World Rhône wines—but, with a distinct "Washington" twist. However, it's the romance, the ritual, and the history of wine that really motivates and inspires her at the end of the day.

Forward-thinking, Mari continues to impress with her wines and she's amassed a loyal following of both heroes and heroines eager to rescue their own bottle (or two, or three!). It's love at first sip, one could say.

TOP: Three of our treasures; Damsel Cellars Syrah, "The Fates" GSM Blend and Cabernet Sauvignon
Photograph by Alex Farias

BELOW LEFT: Our boy Taz sniffing his way through the Syrah rows.
Photograph by Mari Womack

BELOW RIGHT: Getting ready to open the Woodinville tasting room.
Photograph by Sara Womack

COLUMBIA VALLEY SYRAH

GOURMET PAIRINGS

Chef Aaron Tekulve of Seattle-based Surrell created a decadent recipe featuring octopus with smoky bacon, fish sauce caramel, and ramp salsa verde to pair with this flagship Syrah.

TASTING NOTES

A Damsel Cellars signature wine, this Syrah has a purity to its plush texture with alluring ripe blackberry and black currant transitioning to distinct nuances of cured meat, hints of caramel, and black pepper. Medium-bodied with a slight Old World feel, it also pairs beautifully with soft bleu cheeses, triple cream brie, slow-roasted pork shoulder, and herb-encrusted lamb.

WINEMAKER'S INSIGHT

The fruit is sourced from Stillwater Creek Vineyard in Royal City. There are two clones of Syrah blended together in this wine; one with distinct peppery aromatics and heavy spice, and the other with a dominating fruit-forward character. The fruit is de-stemmed, crushed and ferments ferment for approximately seven to 10 days. The wine will remain in 25 percent new French oak for 14 to 16 months before bottling.

AWARDS & DISTINCTIONS

91 points–Wine Enthusiast
Top 20 Wines Under $30, Seattle Met

TECHNICAL DATA

APPELLATION: Columbia Valley
COMPOSITION: 100% Syrah
MATURATION: Aged 16 months in 25% new French oak barrels
CELLARING: Drinks well now, but can be cellared for the next five to seven years

LEARN MORE

Visit our website by scanning the image on the left

DeLille Cellars WOODINVILLE

With an eye toward creating Bordeaux blends from Washington State vineyards, Charles and Greg Lill, Jay Soloff, and celebrated winemaker Chris Upchurch founded DeLille Cellars in 1992. Chris and Jay shared a passion for wine—Chris had been making wine for many years and Jay ran a successful wine brokerage business—and the Lill family owned a hobby farm that became the original winery site. Upon its founding, DeLille Cellars became the fifth winery in Woodinville, and since then has helped establish the state as a premier wine region. The team has always looked to Red Mountain (the home of their estate vineyard, Grand Ciel) and the state's most celebrated vineyards with a focus on blending the powerful, concentrated and structured fruit of Washington to express the unique terroir of the region. With a tradition of excellence and high acclaim, DeLille Cellars was named the "Lafite Rothschild of Washington" and awarded a 5-star/outstanding rating by Robert Parker.

Drawing from French architecture, the Chateau offers guests a charming taste of the Lill family's European heritage. Open for private events only, the Chateau is a beautiful setting for milestone celebrations. Daily wine tastings are held in the quaint Carriage House Tasting Room in Woodinville, where award-winning selections from DeLille's portfolio are available for tastings. Finally, the modern wine lounge in Kirkland, Maison DeLille, offers guests the chance to purchase wine by the glass or bottle, or sample multiple varieties at once with wine flights and light bites.

FACING PAGE: Founding Partner / Executive Winemaker Chris Upchurch (right) and Winemaker Jason Gorski (left) continue to grow the winery's accolades, crafting wines true to the region's terroir.

ABOVE: The Carriage House in Woodinville provides a delightful tasting experience from DeLille's acclaimed portfolio. Favorites among tasters include D2, Chaleur Blanc and Four Flags..
Photographs courtesy of DeLille Cellars

Signature Wines and Wineries of Washington

KASIA WINERY SNOHOMISH

Driven to create art in all aspects of her life—most importantly in winemaking—Kasia Kim, founder and winemaker of Kasia Winery, has crafted a portfolio of wines that each tell a story. From the year and the choice of the varietal to naming the wine and creating its label, each step in the winemaking process is honored with passion and dedication to create a wine experience that pleases the palate while standing out from the crowd.

Since 2014, Kasia Winery has produced wines that are full of personality, with names that include "Open Highway"—an homage to the music of Bon Jovi—"Moxie," and "Off the Hook." The award-winning Open Highway Syrah expresses a spirit of freedom: to go anywhere; moving as quickly or as slowly as you'd like. Off the Hook Dry Rosé is a pale, salmon color Rosé made in the French style with an "off the hook" flavor that consumers love. Finally, Moxie, crafted from Mourvèdre, an arguably challenging varietal, is the epitome of the courage and vigor required to work with the fruit itself, and winemaking as a whole.

FACING PAGE: One of Kasia's favorite things to do is walking the vineyards, feeling the dirt, tasting the grapes, and falling in love with it all.

ABOVE LEFT I hope you enjoy Kasia's wines as much as I enjoy making them.

ABOVE RIGHT Every bottle is signed "by Kasia." It's my promise that this wine reflects my artistic need to create handcrafted wines that are deeply personal.
Photographs by Richard Duval

With a full-hearted approach to winemaking, Kasia only uses the finest grapes from Red Mountain AVA and French oak barrels from top cooperages in France to craft her wines. The result is showcased in each sip, which artfully represents the best of what the terroir offers. When guests visit the tasting room at Kasia Winery and speak with Kasia herself, they know that they're in the presence of an exceptional wine experience inspired by true joie de vivre.

POMUM CELLARS WOODINVILLE

Hailing from the Ribera del Duero region of Spain, Javier Alfonso has been in the wine business almost his whole life. In Spain, his family owned vineyards dating back several generations, but never opened a winery, opting instead to sell fruit to the local village cooperative. With the memories of how challenging and laborious vineyard work can be, Javier initially wanted nothing to do with the wine industry and pursued a degree in mechanical engineering at the University of Washington in Seattle. The choice would lead to two life-changing events: meeting his future wife, Shylah, and the cultivation of a shared passion for wine. The pair soon began exploring the magnificent wines of Washington and the "wine bug" that was so deeply rooted in Javier's genes finally bit. Together, Shylah and Javier began making wine in their home in 2000, and by 2003 were making so much that they could not give it all away. The time had come to get licensed and pursue their dream further.

Pomum Cellars was founded in 2004 by Shylah and Javier Alfonso with a simple philosophy: Make the wine during the growing season by closely working with vineyard partners. Pomum works with the most meticulous growers that own parcels of older vines in unique sites. Each year, Pomum sources fruit from the same blocks, rows, and plants so that Javier, who serves as winemaker, can hone his style and improve the quality of the wine year after year.

Current offerings include a dry Riesling from the historic Upland Vineyards, a steep gravelly hillside in the middle of the Snipes Mountain AVA.

FACING PAGE: Mount Adams as viewed from one of Pomum's Cabernet Franc blocks at Dineen Vineyards in Zillah.

TOP: Pomum Cellars uses exclusively imported Spanish amphorae (called tinajas in Spanish) to craft elegant and age-worthy reds.
Photographs by Richard Duval

Pomum's sublime Chardonnay hails from older vineyards in the Yakima Valley and is crafted for elegance and aging potential. The winery's "Red Wine" is a blend designed to showcase the strength of Bordeaux varieties in Washington State. This wine may be one of the best values in the state as it is blended from the same high-end vineyards touted by the most elite wineries.

Pomum's Tinto Tempranillo epitomizes Javier's passion for this Spanish king of grapes grown in the vineyards of Washington. The beautifully crafted Syrah represents the pinnacle of Washington Syrah; cooler and warmer sites within the Columbia Valley are blended for the perfect combination of the traditional Syrah aroma character coupled with a fresh mouthfeel. Finally, Pomum's signature Shya Red Blend—named for Shylah's childhood nickname—is the winery's interpretation of the apex of Yakima Valley Cabernet Sauvignon.

TOP LEFT: Dineen Tempranillo fruit recently picked waiting to be loaded and driven to Pomum Cellars in Woodinville.
Photograph by Richaed Duval

BELOW LEFT: Javier Alfonso and his workhorse hand-driven basket press at Pomum Cellars in Woodinville WA.
Photograph by Richaed Duval

ABOVE: Winemaker Javier Alfonso inspecting old vine Estate Cabernet Sauvignon and discussing the growing season with vineyard founder and manager Chuck Fiola.
Photograph by Amanda Miles

SHYA RED CABERNET SAUVIGNON

GOURMET PAIRINGS

Yakima Valley Cabernet Sauvignon shines for its freshness and elegance. Yes, it can be paired with steak, but the Shya Red will also match perfectly with lighter roasted meats and even richer seafood dishes.

TASTING NOTES

Our Shya Red Cabernet Sauvignon is intended to showcase the characteristics of this king of grapes. Typically a bit of Merlot and sometimes Petit Verdot will be included to add richness and complexity to the blend. The dark crimson wine shows aromas of black cherry and dark currant with a fascinating spice note. Fresh and juicy dark fruit flavors are followed by round and impeccably integrated tannins. Long and alluring, this wine is above all, greatly balanced.

WINEMAKER'S INSIGHT

Our Shya Red Cabernet is crafted from older, nearly forgotten vineyards, including Konnowac Vineyard, with some of the oldest Petit Verdot and Malbec in the state, and Morrison Vineyard with Cabernet vines dating back to 1968. We allow the vineyards to craft the wine, and in the cellar, we guide the process through its natural stages of fermentation. Grapes are destemmed into small open top tanks, and fermentation occurs naturally without chemical additions or harsh mechanical processes. A slow, traditional basket press, used for all our red wines, yields only the highest quality wine.

AWARDS AND DISTINCTIONS

Consistently favored by consumers, sommeliers, and buyers across the world for its deft expression of terroir.

TECHNICAL DATA

APPELLATION: Yakima Valley
COMPOSITION: 100% Cabernet Sauvignon
MATURATION: Aged 18 months in French oak (25% new); matured in bottle for an additional 30 months
CELLARING: Perfect five years after vintage, peaking after 10 years

LEARN MORE

Visit our website by scanning the image to left

QUILCEDA CREEK SNOHOMISH

Quilceda Creek founders Alex and Jeannette Golitzin have relentlessly pursued their goal of crafting world-class Cabernet Sauvignon since establishing the winery in 1978. What began as a pioneering effort in the family's garage in the early days of Washington winemaking has grown into a second-generation winery now led by the Golitzins' son Paul. With a commitment to quality that rivals his parents, Paul has focused the winery's attention on its greatest asset, the vineyards of the Columbia Valley. Today, the wines are among the most sought-after Cabernet Sauvignons in America.

It could be said that the Golitzins' family heritage predestined the wines to greatness. A relative of Prince Lev Sergervich Golitzin, acclaimed winemaker to Russian Czar Nicholas II, the French-born Alex lived in Paris until 1946. His family immigrated to San Francisco, and throughout his youth, Alex regularly visited Napa Valley and his maternal uncle, André Tchelistcheff, legendary Napa Valley vintner at Beaulieu Vineyards. Despite his lineage, Alex's path to winemaking took shape slowly. A chemical engineer by training, Alex moved the family from California to Washington State in 1967 to accept a job at Scott Paper. In the mid-1970s, the couple's interest in high-quality wines led Alex and Jeannette to begin experimenting with a few barrels. Encouraged by what they tasted, they soon felt prepared to establish a small winery. With Alex as winemaker and Jeannette as sales director, Quilceda Creek produced its first commercially released Cabernet Sauvignon in 1979. The wines earned critical acclaim from the start, and the winery continued to grow throughout the 1980s. By 1994, Alex was ready to retire from his day job at Scott Paper to focus on the winery exclusively.

FACING PAGE: The Estate of Quilceda Creek in Snohomish.
Photograph courtesy of Quilceda Creek

TOP: Quilceda Creek Cabernet Sauvignon wines and red blends consistently receive critical acclaim. *Wine Advocate* has awarded six 100-point ratings.
Photograph by Keith Megay Photography

CABERNET SAUVIGNON COLUMBIA VALLEY

GOURMET PAIRINGS
Pairs well with ribeye steak, lightly-seasoned filet mignon, or rack of lamb.

TASTING NOTES
Packed with floral aromas and flavors of blackberry, blueberry, black cherry, and plum fruit, intertwined with nuances of cacao nib, anise, soy, forest floor, and minerals, the Cabernet Sauvignon Columbia Valley is complex but approachable. Its silky texture shines throughout, leaving a lasting finish.

WINEMAKER'S INSIGHT
Great wine starts in the vineyard. In hot growing seasons, the winery uses custom-designed overhead misters to cool the fruit on the most extreme days. Nearly all of the grapes ripen under perfect 70-degree Fahrenheit temperatures in October, giving the winemaker concentrated grapes, full of flavor. This Cabernet Sauvignon is sourced from the Champoux, Palengat, and Wallula Vineyards. The wine matured in new French oak barrels for 20 months to create a complex but silky wine.

AWARDS AND DISTINCTIONS
100 points–Wine Advocate

TECHNICAL DATA
APPELLATION: Columbia Valley
COMPOSITION: 100% Cabernet Sauvignon
MATURATION: Aged 20 months in 100% new French oak
CELLARING: Wonderful at release; cellars for 20+ years

VISIT OUR STORE

Buy this wine by scanning image on left

TOP: Cabernet Sauvignon grapes growing in the Wallula Vineyards in the Horse Heaven Hills AVA.

BELOW: The Champoux Vineyards, Alderdale, Washington, in the Horse Heaven Hills AVA.
Photographs by David Sproul, District 4 Creative

He and son Paul, who joined the winery full-time in 1992, shared winemaking responsibilities. The two proved to be a formidable team.

"A great bottle of wine is one that keeps your interest from the first glass to the last, leaving you wanting more," says Paul. He brings an unwavering commitment to the pursuit of excellence in every detail of grape growing, fermentation, cellar management, blending and bottling. Under Paul's leadership, *Wine Advocate* has awarded Quilceda Creek six 100-point ratings over a 13-year period, a phenomenal accomplishment. Alongside Paul, John Ware, vice president and general manager, ensures all the inner workings and management of the winery and vineyards remain

consistent and of the utmost quality. With the belief that great wine begins in great vineyards, Quilceda Creek set its sights on acquiring a handful of top vineyard sites in the mid-1990s, a move that catapulted the wines to a new level of excellence. In 1997, the winery formed a partnership with Paul Champoux and a few other marquee wineries to purchase Mercer Ranch Vineyard (renamed Champoux Vineyard) in the Horse Heaven Hills AVA. Quilceda Creek became majority owners of Champoux in 2014. One of the oldest vineyards in Washington, Champoux is considered by many Washington winemakers to be the best Cabernet Sauvignon site in the state. Buoyed by the quality of Champoux Cabernet, the winery continued its Horse Heaven Hills expansion, purchasing a four-and-one-half-acre site adjacent to Champoux Vineyard in 2006. The vineyard is named Palengat, Jeannette's maiden name. Other Horse Heaven Hills non-estate vineyard sources include the south-facing Lake Wallula Vineyards, overlooking the Columbia River.

Recognizing the importance of diverse vineyard holdings, the family planted the 17-acre Galitzine Vineyard estate in 2001 in the Red Mountain AVA, a small but highly acclaimed growing region also recognized for outstanding Cabernet Sauvignon. The vineyard is named after Alex's father who revised the spelling

TOP: The Great Room at Quilceda Creek's Estate in Snohomish provides a relaxing setting for enjoying world-class wines.

BELOW: Quilceda Creek's age-worthy wines are sought after by collectors and equally prized by enthusiasts who enjoy the wines on release.
Photographs by John Kaplan Photography

GALITZINE VINEYARD
CABERNET SAUVIGNON RED MOUNTAIN

GOURMET PAIRINGS

Pairs well with braised beef short ribs, roasted tomato and goat cheese tart, or wild arugula salad.

TASTING NOTES

An exotic and rich wine, the Cabernet Sauvignon is filled with aromas and flavors of blackberry and black cherry fruit, with nuances of chocolate, forest floor, and minerals.

WINEMAKER'S INSIGHT

The Galitzine Vineyard Cabernet Sauvignon captures the best of what Red Mountain has to offer. Composed primarily of Cabernet Sauvignon from the Galitzine Vineyard, small amounts of Cabernet Sauvignon from other vineyards are blended in to add complexity and aroma. After harvest and fermentation, the wine was aged in 100 percent French oak for 20 months.

AWARDS AND DISTINCTIONS

100 points–Wine Advocate

TECHNICAL DATA

APPELLATION: Red Mountain
COMPOSITION: 100% Cabernet Sauvignon
MATURATION: Aged 20 months in 100% new French oak
CELLARING: Beautiful upon release and cellars well for 20+ years

LEARN MORE

Learn more about this wine and our winery by scanning the image on the left

PALENGAT PROPRIETARY RED WINE
COLUMBIA VALLEY

GOURMET PAIRINGS

Pairs beautifully with grilled meats, portabella mushroom burgers, and roasted root vegetables.

TASTING NOTES

The highly expressive blend features violet infused plum and crème de cassis fruit that coats the entire palate, with accents of five-spice powder, black truffles, vanilla, and minerals.

WINEMAKER'S INSIGHT

Palengat Proprietary Red Wine is a Cabernet Sauvignon-forward blend that also features Merlot and Cabernet Franc. Aged for 20 months in new French oak, the wine showcases the unique qualities of the Horse Heaven Hills AVA and includes expressive fruit from Champoux, Palengat, Lake Wallula, and Wallula Gap Vineyards.

AWARDS AND DISTINCTIONS

96 points–Wine Advocate

TECHNICAL DATA

APPELLATION: Horse Heaven Hills
COMPOSITION: Primarily Cabernet Sauvignon, with Merlot and Cabernet Franc
MATURATION: Aged 20 months in 100% new French oak
CELLARING: Delicious upon release; cellaring for a decade or more

VISIT OUR STORE

Buy this wine by scanning image on left

TOP: Another view of the decor in the Great Room at Quilceda Creek.

ABOVE: Stylistic art and sculpture beautifully accessorize the Great Room at Quilceda Creek.
Photograph by John Kaplan Photography

of his last name from Galitzine to Golitzin after immigrating to the US following WWII. From the beginning, the grapes have been sensational, prompting the winery to release its first vineyard-designated Galitzine Cabernet Sauvignon in 2004.

In 2006, Robert M. Parker, Jr.'s *Wine Advocate* wrote, "There isn't a Cabernet producer with this winery's track record for consistency," and bestowed two perfect 100-point ratings on both the 2002 and 2003 vintages of Cabernet Sauvignon. Two years later, the winery received another 100 point rating from Mr. Parker's publication for the 2005 Cabernet Sauvignon and again for the 2007 Cabernet Sauvignon. Wine Advocate followed these ratings with two more perfect scores for both the 2014 Cabernet Sauvignon and 2014 Cabernet Sauvignon, Galitzine Vineyard in 2017. Wine Spectator weighed in too, naming Quilceda Creek to its prestigious annual "Top Ten Wines in the World" list three times in the last decade (2003 #2, 2010 #10 and 2012 #2). Most recently, Wine Advocate named Quilceda Creek "Best Washington State Winery 2017" at its Extraordinary Winery Awards for the Americas gala. The honor is presented to one winery in each major wine region of the world that "stands qualitatively above all others," according to Wine Advocate editor-in-chief Lisa Perrotti-Brown, MW.

ABOVE & LEFT: Since its founding in 1978, Quilceda Creek has dedicated itself to world-class Cabernet Sauvignon.
Photographs by Keith Megay Photography

CVR COLUMBIA VALLEY RED WINE

GOURMET PAIRINGS

Pairs beautifully with roasted or grilled lamb and blue cheese wedge salads.

TASTING NOTES

The Quilceda Creek CVR is a captivating blend of all vineyard sites, filled with satisfying red and blue fruits, smoke, spice, and minerals.

WINEMAKER'S INSIGHT

Crafted primarily from Cabernet Sauvignon, the blend is best enjoyed for 15 years after release.

AWARDS AND DISTINCTIONS

94 points – Wine Advocate

TECHNICAL DATA

APPELLATION: Columbia Valley

COMPOSITION: Primarily Cabernet Sauvignon, with Merlot, Cabernet Franc, and Petit Verdot

MATURATION: Aged in 100% French oak

CELLARING: Elegant upon release and cellars well for 15+ years

LEARN MORE

Learn more about this wine and our winery by scanning the image on the left

ROBERT RAMSAY CELLARS WOODINVILLE

Traditional style, food-friendly Rhone wines are the hallmark of Robert Ramsay Cellars, where subtleties and nuances in traditionally-crafted wine are showcased. Here, one does not find the big, bold flavors characteristic of wineries of California, but wines that are suited for refined palates—those that crave a balanced acidity and appreciate complexity without a monolithic punch of oaky flavors. Owner and winemaker Robert "Bob" Ramsay Harris founded Robert Ramsay Cellars on the principles for his great-uncle and namesake, Mason Ramsay, was known. Mason mentored Bob's father for years and stories of Mason's life are still being passed down to new generations, but they all have a common thread: treat others with respect, work with and for the community, and don't be afraid to get your hands dirty, literally in some cases as Mason was a shop teacher and rancher. It made sense then that Bob would pay homage to this great man when it came to naming the winery, where getting your hands dirty is a daily activity.

Gifted with a fine-tuned nose—and a mom who went back to school as an adult and left her husband and boys to figure things out for themselves at mealtimes—Bob taught himself to cook. From an early age, food and the way flavors mixed became very important to him. Years later, while on break during college, he met and worked for a man who owned an extensive wine cellar that focused on European wines. The friends would cook together and share a bottle of wine that, most of the time, impressed Bob's now sophisticated palate. At one such get-together, he looked at the wine and thought, "This didn't just happen. Someone built this wine and made it happen. I want to build something like this."

FACING PAGE: Spring showers and sunlight over the Dineen Vineyards in the Yakima Valley.
Photograph by Richard Duval

ABOVE: Owner/Winemaker Robert Ramsay behind the tasting bar at Robert Ramsay Cellars in Woodinville.
Photograph by Keith Magae

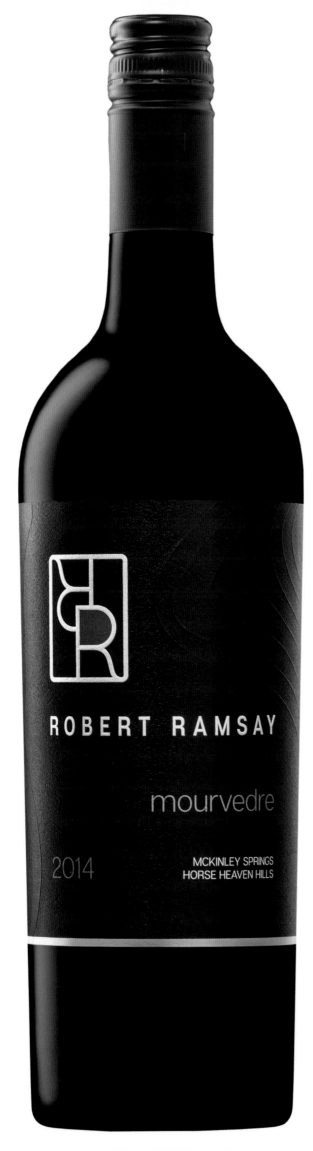

MCKINLEY SPRINGS HORSE HEAVEN HILLS MOURVÈDRE

GOURMET PAIRINGS

The wine's spice profile and medium body make it a great complement to your favorite steak as well as dishes on the lighter side: salmon and fresh vegetable pasta.

TASTING NOTES

Mourvèdre hails from Southern France and Spain and is known for its spicy nose, meaty notes, and rustic profile. Rough and earthy, like its terroir, the McKinley Springs Horse Heaven Hills Mourvèdre offers a peppery nose of intense and focused aromas. A rich mouthfeel of leather and tobacco carries you to the finish. We have been bottling this wine as a single varietal since 2007.

WINEMAKER'S INSIGHT

Here in the New World, Mourvèdre has gained popularity among red wine enthusiasts. Often used as a blending grape, here in our McKinley Springs Horse Heaven Hills Mourvèdre, the fruit gets to take center stage. Deep in the Horse Heaven Hills grows McKinley Springs, a vineyard first planted with wine grapes in 1995. The soils are deep, sandy loams atop broken basalt—prime conditions for heat-loving Rhone varietals.

AWARDS AND DISTINCTIONS

90 points – Wine Enthusiast

TECHNICAL DATA

APPELLATION: Horse Heaven Hills
COMPOSITION: 100% Mourvèdre
MATURATION: Aged 2 years in barrel before bottling
CELLARING: Wonderful upon release and ages well for up to 10 years

LEARN MORE

Visit our website by scanning image on left

Fast-forward to September 2001, when Bob, who had majored in entrepreneurial studies and worked in the software industry realized that his current career wasn't meant to be his final one. He quit his job, traveled the world, and went out to start a winery. With a business plan in hand and trusted winemaker friends to call upon, Bob started his first winery in 2002. A few years later, in 2005, Robert Ramsay Cellars was founded, and Bob credits the help of great winemakers—some of whom he met by chance in the vineyards—as one of the most important reasons for his success. "I never screwed up too badly," he jokes, but the lessons he learned have, without a doubt, contributed to the portfolio of traditional-style wines for which Robert Ramsay Cellars has become known. With an eye out for the perfect conditions to make a once-in-a-lifetime wine, Bob focuses on making exemplary wine that makes wine connoisseurs and beginning wine lovers alike exclaim, "I want more of that!"

Moderately priced—some would say underpriced for their quality—and always food-friendly, Robert Ramsay Cellars

TOP: The iconic Chapel at Red Willow Vineyard.

RIGHT: Some of the oldest Syrah plantings in Washington state come from the Red Willow Vineyard.
Photograph by Richard Duval

wines have an Old-World character often missed in New World selections. The critics agree. Mason's Red, named in honor of Mason Ramsay, received a Double Gold Medal and the Mourvèdre received a Gold Medal at the Seattle Wine Awards. The Par la Mer blend received 90 points from Wine Spectator, while the same publication has awarded the Dineen Syrah 91 points. Ultimately, Bob and the entire team at Robert Ramsay Cellars say the number one rule of wine drinking is to drink what you like. Fortunately for visitors to the winery and the Queen Anne Tasting Room, there's something for every taste.

When guests arrive at the winery, they're immediately treated like friends. During tasting hours, the tasting room features a subset of wines set aside for the location. Located in the Woodinville Warehouse District, the winery offers a laid-back, friendly experience no matter your knowledge level about wine. The winery team believes there's nothing quite like sharing the joy of wine, and they're always ready to tell you all about Robert Ramsay Cellars likes to craft it. When asked, they'll also recommend their favorite varietals.

TOP: The iconic chapel overlooks the Red Willow Vineyard–the westernmost vineyard in the Yakima Valley.
Photograph by Richard Duval

RIGHT: Enjoy a flight of Robert Ramsay wines at their tasting bar near downtown Seattle.
Photograph by Keith Magae

UPLAND VINEYARD
SNIPES MOUNTAIN GRENACHE

GOURMET PAIRINGS

Grenache is exceptionally food-friendly, so it will pair well with just about anything. Try it with slow-cooked pork, lamb, poultry, or gourmet cheese and salad options.

TASTING NOTES

The nose is reminiscent of a field of raspberry in summer; at once earthy and fresh. A juicy palate reveals hints of cranberry, while white pepper flavors mingle with mineral tones and great acidity to complete the wine. Light and crisp, the finish lingers delightfully and will bring you back for more.

WINEMAKER'S INSIGHT

Grenache is among the most widely planted varietals across the globe and is grown extensively in Southern France and Spain, as well as parts of the United States. The varietal loves a hot and dry climate, accompanied by long growing days. Upland Vineyard provides these conditions on its steep south-facing slope above the Yakima River.

AWARDS & DISTINCTIONS

Bronze Medal – San Francisco Chronicle Wine Competition

TECHNICAL DATA

APPELLATION: Snipes Mountain
COMPOSITION: 100% Grenache
MATURATION: Aged 2 years in barrel before bottling
CELLARING: May be cellared for 20 years or longer

VISIT OUR STORE

Order this and other wines at our store by scanning the image on the left

COLUMBIA VALLEY SYRAH

GOURMET PAIRINGS

Grilled meats like steak, lamb, and darker foul provide the perfect pairing for the medium acidity and tannin of our Columbia Valley Syrah.

TASTING NOTES

Our Columbia Valley Syrah offers dark fruit on the nose, with hints of licorice. A rich, evolving flavor of blackberry and plum with chocolate notes carries this wine to its finish. Medium acidity and smooth tannins make this wine exceptionally food friendly.

WINEMAKER'S INSIGHT

Syrah is among the darkest of red wines and as such can be a full-bodied wine. By blending fruit from three vineyards, Dineen, McKinley Springs, and Phinny Hill, our Columbia Valley Syrah captures the best of what these three vineyards have to offer without being too heavy. Together, the fruit from these three vineyards brings a purity to the varietal.

AWARDS AND DISTINCTIONS

89 points – Wine Enthusiast

TECHNICAL DATA

APPELLATION: Columbia Valley
COMPOSITION: Predominantly Syrah with a minuscule percentage of Viognier
MATURATION: Aged 2 years in barrel before bottling
CELLARING: Delicious upon release and can be stored for up to 10 years

LEARN MORE

Visit our website by scanning image on left

The Queen Anne Tasting Room, located on Queen Anne Avenue in Seattle, offers daily happy hour specials as well as small bites: sandwiches, tapas, charcuterie boards, and other small plates created to complement the wines. While less of a tasting room experience and more like a small café, the Queen Anne Tasting Room offers wine flights, so visitors can experience multiple wines in one sitting.

Wine Club members enjoy a 50 percent discount for their initial shipment. After that, distributions occur three times a year, and members can choose any wines they'd like, or simply receive new releases by default. With multiple tiers available, 10 to 20 percent off all purchases, and a complimentary tasting for members and their guests, membership is—like everything else at Robert Ramsay Cellars—focused on giving wine aficionados an amazing experience.

TOP: Cinsault and Grenache are two of the five main Rhone Red Varietals made at Robert Ramsay Cellars

RIGHT: Mourvèdre is the King grape from the French wine making region of Bandol. Robert Ramsay bottles Mourvedre on its own as well as creates a Bandol inspired blend called Par la Mer.
Photographs by Keith Magae

SIGILLO CELLARS SNOQUALMIE

Little did Sigillo Cellars' father-and-son team Mike Seal and Ryan Seal realize, but their casual golf-course conversation with former winemaker Steve Bailey in 2005 would turn out to be a whole lot more than just small talk.

Five years after that day on the putting green—and many bottles of wine made (and lessons learned) in Steve's garage—Mike and Ryan officially founded Sigillo, named for the Italian translation of their last name. Joined by partners, Scott and Christie Hussey, they wanted to share their passion for good wine with more than just their closest friends. The first year, they produced 400 cases, then tripled their production by 2012. They currently put "Sigillo"—their "seal" of approval—on more than 4,000 cases of Bordeaux and Rhône-style wines garnered from 65 tons of premium eastern Washington fruit including varietals from Red Mountain, Wahluke Slope, Yakima Valley, Rattlesnake Hills, and Columbia Valley AVAs.

Some of those wines include their signature Bordeaux blends such as the Confluence and Sunset labels. Named for the winery's proximity to the confluence of the three forks of the Snoqualmie River, Confluence is made of four traditional varietals, including Cabernet Sauvignon, Merlot, Cabernet Franc, and Petit Verdot. Sunset is offered in honor of the winery's tasting room location at the hundred-year-old Sunset Theatre in the heart of downtown Snoqualmie. As the name would suggest, Sunset is an "old world" blend with Carmenere added to the famous five. One of the favorite southern Rhône-style blends is Relativity, inspired by Einstein's Theory, and offering a harmonious mix of aromas and flavors. Tempranillo from the Wahluke Slope, made in the true Spanish style, is another top pick.

FACING PAGE: Ryan Seal, left, pulls some barrel samples as fellow Sigillo owners, Mike Seal, Christie Hussey, Scott Hussey, and Cande Collins prepare for an upcoming bottling of their 2016 wines.

TOP: Sigillo owners celebrate the awesome taste of our latest Malbec. (L-R) Mike Seal, Cande Collins, Christie Hussey, Scott Hussey, Ryan Seal.
Photographs by Kristy Ray Photography

VIOGNIER

GOURMET PAIRINGS
Delicious paired with roasted carrots in a citrus-spice dressing, topped with pea shoots and sesame.

TASTING NOTES
With notes of lemongrass, green apple, pear and honey, the wine is very typical of the traditional Rhône-style wines. It has a great nose and long finish on the palate.

WINEMAKER'S INSIGHT
Our Viognier quality starts with a great grower: Lonesome Spring Ranch Vineyards. Each vintage is a bit different, of course, so vineyard management is adjusted to coordinate each year independently. Our Viognier is whole cluster pressed and fermented in stainless tanks, maintaining a somewhat cooler fermentation temperature.

AWARDS & DISTINCTIONS
Silver Medal–Savor NW Wine Awards

TECHNICAL DATA
APPELLATION: Yakima Valley
COMPOSITION: 100% Viognier

PAIRINGS RECIPE

We are happy to share our pairings recipe above. Simply scan the image on the left for the complete preparation instructions and enjoy!

A visit to Sigillo Cellars is very much tied to the historic area of Snoqualmie; it's something that is very important to Mike and Ryan and one of the reasons they selected the Sunset Theatre for their family-friendly tasting room there. The beautifully restored building has plenty of historical charm in its preserved high ceiling, projection booth, entry and ticket window. An outside deck highlights the gorgeous views of the famous Mt. Si—many even stop by Sigillo after making the 4,000-foot climb for a well-deserved glass of wine. Light fare and live entertainment encourages visitors to stay for more than just a sip.

Of course, in addition to this full-bodied wine experience, a visit to Sigillo might just be motivated by finding out the identity of Mike and wife Cande Collins' secret (and famous!) winemaking coach.

Just as Sigillo Cellars is woven into the fabric of downtown Snoqualmie, the winery donates their tasting room to

TOP: Sigillo's Snoqualmie Tasting Room is in the heart of Downtown's Historic Sunset Theatre.

RIGHT: Sigillo events include weekly visits by local and regional musicians featuring lots of original music.
Photographs by Kristy Ray Photography

many charitable fundraising causes including the YMCA and Snoqualmie Valley School Foundation. They also produce an annual summer barbecue and wine party for their wine club members called Sigillo in the Park, and just recently added a winter fete called Sigillo on the Train, as tourism visits to Sigillo are simply not complete without seeing the historic Snoqualmie Train Museum and the famous Snoqualmie Falls. With these splendid events, it's just another way that Sigillo can give back to the community while celebrating the joys of fine wine.

TOP: Sigillo Malbec is picked with care at Weinbau Vineyards

BELOW LEFT: Pouring the Sunset blend. It may very each year, but will always contain Cabernet Sauvignon, Cabernet Franc, Merlot, Malbec, Petit Verdot and Carménère.

BELOW RIGHT: Sigillo owners relax around the cozy fireplace in its Snoqualmie tasting room.
Photographs by Kristy Ray Photography

MALBEC

GOURMET PAIRINGS

Malbec-steamed mussels with chorizo and crispy sausage in a chimichurri sauce is a delightful way to integrate this wine into a dish

TASTING NOTES

Our Malbec is sourced from the Weinbau Vineyard in the Wahluke Slope AVA, one of the many suburb vineyards of Sagemoor Vineyards. Malbec does well when the fruit is allowed good exposure to the sun. Careful vertical shoot positioning give the vines direct sunlight all morning along with a nice layer of leaf protection later in the day once the grapes have warmed up to ambient temperature.

WINEMAKER'S INSIGHT

Malbec ripens to a deep, dense color with broad flavor potential. Maintaining that character is the goal of our winemaker. The fruit is allowed to "saigner," the French word for bleed, for up to two to three days before fermentation is started. Maintaining a consistent, medium temperature fermentation is important to our style.

AWARDS & DISTINCTIONS

Double Gold–SavorNW Wine Awards.

TECHNICAL DATA

APPELLATION: Wahluke Slope
COMPOSITION: 100% Malbec
MATURATION: Aged 18-19 months in 50% new French oak barrels
CELLARING: Delicious upon release, but expect exceptional depth in two to three years

PAIRINGS RECIPE

We are happy to share our pairings recipe above. Simply scan the image on the left for the complete preparation instructions and enjoy!

Soos Creek Wine Cellars KENT

Hard work and dedication are long-time companions of David Larsen, winemaker and founder of Soos Creek Wine Cellars. A former marathon runner, David's inspiration to found his winery began with a trip to Europe after he completed his active duty with the Marine Corps. While in Europe, he developed an appreciation for wine and discovered that he was fascinated by how it enhanced a meal. When he returned home, he began making blackberry wine as a hobby and even shared it with his wife, Cecile, on their first date. In the 1970s, the pair traveled to Napa Valley in a trip that planted the seed for starting their winery.

His love of wine continued in the following years as he worked in The Boeing Company's finance department and soon joined the Boeing Employees Winemaking Club. At the time, the Washington wine industry was still forming, with very few wineries in the state. But these early wineries, which included Leonetti, Woodward Canyon, and Quilceda Creek, provided the final example that David needed to make the jump from corporate America to the vineyard. Soos Creek started small—in David's garage, in fact—and grew to today's maximum production of 2,500 cases annually. Drawing upon his background in finance, David has kept his overhead low with creative partnerships like trading a few bottles of wine for label designs, and as a result, Soos Creek wines are among the best priced in the region.

FACING PAGE: Pouring a sample at annual open house.

TOP: All 15 vintages of the Artist Series from 2001 - 2015. *Photographs by Richard Duval*

As a winemaker, David focuses on the fruit first with an exclusive production of red wine made from Bordeaux grape varietals. He bases his winemaking decisions on taste, rather than making wine by the numbers, and it shows.

The flavors of the Soos Creek wines are exquisite, all with a stylistic trademark of bright, fresh, red fruit flavors and lithe tannins. Approachable with enough structure for the long haul, Soos Creek wines impress even the most discerning palates. David sources grapes from Champoux Vineyard in the Horse Heaven Hills AVA; Ciel du Cheval Vineyard and Klipsun Vineyard in the Red Mountain AVA; Sagemoor Family of Vineyards in the Columbia Valley AVA; Dineen Vineyard in the Rattlesnake Hills AVA; and other vineyards in the state. From the bright, ruby-red Palisades Merlot to the Stampede Pass Cabernet Franc and beyond, Soos Creek wines are the epitome of what Washington offers, delivered by a winemaker determined to produce fine wines with each passing year.

TOP LEFT: Assistant Winemaker, Landon Gibson; Owner/Winemaker, David Larsen; Cellar Master, Mark Stevens.
Photograph by Richaed Duval

TOP RIGHT: Portrait of the Larsen family: Cecile, David Sr., Jeff, David Jr., and Kevin.
Photograph by Richaed Duval

BELOW LEFT: Customers attending annual open house release party.
Photograph by Steve Beckley

BELOW RIGHT: Founder, David Larsen standing behind a basket press inside the winery.
Photograph by Richaed Duval

CIEL DU CHEVAL VINEYARD BORDEAUX BLEND

GOURMET PAIRINGS

Pairs well with a medium-rare, lightly seasoned New York steak with mushrooms and mashed potatoes.

TASTING NOTES

The Ciel du Cheval Vineyard Bordeaux Blend is a bright, deep ruby-red blend. It features inviting, fruit-driven aromas of raspberry, blackberry, boysenberry, pie cherry, licorice, and minerals. Sweet, lush, and fully-ripe flavors blend with excellent depth to the wine's blueberry and dark chocolate flavors.

WINEMAKER'S INSIGHT

The grapes sourced for the blend are from vines that are up to 35 years old. Whole berry fermentation is done using native yeast after a four-day cold soak in open-top fermenters. The cap is punched down by hand twice a day, and the must is gently pressed into 100% French oak barrels.

AWARDS AND DISTINCTIONS

Consistently high scores (90+ points) from all major wine critics

TECHNICAL DATA

APPELLATION: Red Mountain

COMPOSITION: 65% Cabernet Sauvignon, 20% Merlot, 15% Cabernet Franc

MATURATION: Eighteen to 20 months in 100% French oak barrels and another year after bottling

CELLARING: Drinkable upon release with a 20-year track record of aging beautifully

LEARN MORE

Visit our website by scanning the image to left

STRUCTURE CELLARS SEATTLE

FACING PAGE: The whole family, Brian, Valentine, Brandee and Nubbin, sits in front of a 16' tall painting by Brandee, "Grape Bones," in their very first tasting room.

ABOVE: Structure's first tasting space, The BLUEPRINT Room, serves up the ever approachable "Everyday Special" Blue Label wines, and old school hip-hop music keeps things casual.
Photograph by Christophe Serviers

Go big or go home isn't just a saying at Structure Cellars, it's a way of life. Owners Brandee Slosar and Brian Grasso—B Squared for short—started their winery based on a shared passion for great wine. It didn't begin that way, though. Brian was more of a gregarious "vodka guy" with two decades working in the fine dining industry. His appreciation for wine was just beginning. Brandee, the lifelong wine lover, had abandoned aspirations of being an architect and was a wardrobe and set stylist.

Brian describes the day he realized that he wanted to be a winemaker as the second best in his life (second only to his wedding day). After a "field trip" to a winery with his restaurant group, the light went on. He was going to be a winemaker, and nothing was going to stand in his way. He enrolled in Seattle's NW Wine Academy and began internships at Darby Winery, Sparkman Cellars, and Baer Winery in Woodinville while learning the craft.

In 2008 they made their first barrel, 100 percent Destiny Ridge Syrah. Its quality surprised the couple from the first sip, and they hoped they had something special. As Brian continued to learn the skills from some of the state's iconic winemakers, the couple bought their first home, a real "fixer-upper." One day, when Brandee was working on the house (which had been torn down to the studs), she found herself second-guessing this decision to undertake such a huge project while Brian was still working at his restaurant job, interning, and making wine. During the mayhem, the eternal optimist Brian brought out a bottle of the 2008 Syrah (their first wine) and said, "You know, this house is a lot like this wine, it's got good bones...good structure."

"BAUHAUS" SYRAH

GOURMET PAIRINGS

The flavors of grilled lamb and fresh hearty herbs are the a perfect pairing to "Bauhaus" Syrah's full bodied, fruit forward richness.

TASTING NOTES

Look for black and white pepper, fennel seed, raspberry jam, thyme, and bacon fat on the nose. This complex wine is perfect for those who love to savor earthy notes, a generous fruit-driven mid-palate, and a complex, smoky tannic finish.

WINEMAKER'S INSIGHT

This is the perfect expression of Brian's favorite varietal! Bauhaus Syrah captures the essence of winemaking that honors the art of the grape. From a deep blue-violet emerge silky tannins and balanced acids—this is truly an expressive wine. Little intervention goes into making our Syrah; we prefer to invest in the best fruit possible and then let the grapes ferment and mature largely on their own.

AWARDS & DISTINCTIONS

92 points–Wine Enthusiast

TECHNICAL DATA

APPELLATION: Columbia Valley
COMPOSITION: 90% Syrah with 10% Malbec
MATURATION: 19 months seasoned French Oak
CELLARING: Approachable now, will peak in 4-6 years.

GRILLED LAMB RECIPE

Enjoy our special grilled lamb recipe pictured above by scanning the image on the left

At that moment, the name for their future winery was clear: Structure Cellars. Today, Structure Cellars wines occupy a place of prestige in Washington. The portfolio includes the winery's Everyday-Special Blue label wines, White label "Foundation" wines, and Brown label 100 percent single vineyard "Structure+Terroir" wines. Brandee's passion for architecture never died and is evident on each label of Structure wine.

The perfect example of Brian's approach to winemaking would be unpretentious, approachable, and food friendly. No matter which label graces the bottle you choose, the same simple winemaking style is evident in all Structure Cellars wines. Being true to varietal, Brian often takes a non-interventionist approach to the fruit, allowing the best of what each grape has to offer to come through brilliantly on its own.

From Thursday through Sunday, Brian and Brandee are at their Seattle tasting rooms, personally circulating among the guests and refilling glasses for those who just can't get enough

TOP: Guests enjoy the "Foundation" and "Structure+Terroir" wines by the soft glow of the 8'x17' Light Wall, which is flanked by a fireplace and a towering 20' long steel Wine Wall which holds 768 bottles of wine.

RIGHT: Brian Grasso and Brandee Slosar in The CELLAR, in front of the Wine Wall.
Photograph by Christophe Serviers

of Structure Cellars' offerings. In the lux industrial surroundings of the CELLAR, Brandee can often be found at the base of the 20-foot long steel wine wall which holds 64 cases of wine, and singing the praises of her favorite wine, the "Foundation" Cabernet Franc. Eclectic chairs and a fireplace add an artsy vibe to the space, while a room divider constructed of an aluminum skeleton and 3,000 LED lights and covered in theater fabric, creates an intimate glow, especially a night when the feature can be seen from the front windows.

Brian chills in the BLUEPRINT tasting room, playing old school hip-hop, introducing guests to his favorite—"Bauhaus" Syrah (any Syrah really) —and waxing poetic about how he approaches each wine. Large, soft gray couches invite you to have a seat, and the walls crafted from deconstructed barrel staves, infuse the back tasting room with a casual vibe. A 16-foot-tall painting, "Grape Bones," painted by Brandee hangs on one wall, colorfully depicts the beauty of the simple grape stem.

TOP: The Structure Family of wines feature the "Everyday Special" Blue Label Wines, the White Label "Foundation" Wine Series, the Brown Label "Structure+Terroir" single vineyard, 100 percent varietal, tribute to the vineyard wines, and the elusive Graphite Labels - unique wines with a production of only 30 cases per year.
Photograph by Christophe Serviers

RIGHT: Crushing 200 cases of Syrah with a small bladder press has expanded to 2,500 cases and four distinct label categories of approachable, food friendly, varietally sound wines in 2018.
Photograph by Kevin Mueller

"FOUNDATION" CABERNET FRANC

GOURMET PAIRINGS

Perfect with wine-soaked spaghetti, with roasted mushrooms and pancetta, as well as game birds – especially duck, pork belly, and turkey with cranberry sauce. Cheese: Chevré, Feta + Camembert.

TASTING NOTES

On the nose, look for blueberry, raspberry, sage, thyme, wet slate, and freshly turned earth. "Foundation" Cabernet Franc's amazing softness and smoothness on the palate simply delight. Blueberry, lavender, thyme, and sawdust come through, and tannins are never too punchy. The finish holds up this complex wine with grace and balance. If ever there was a wine to be savored, it's this one.

WINEMAKER'S INSIGHT

Fruit sourced from Stillwater Creek, Destiny Ridge, and Upland Vineyard was brought together to craft the medium tannin structure of this wine. The fruit remains on the vine longer for this wine than our other offerings, to give it a chance to develop to its full potential, which reminds us of fall in Seattle—a mix of wet earth, rain on cement, and dry leaves…our version of heaven.

AWARDS AND DISTINCTIONS

91 points–Wine Enthusiast

TECHNICAL DATA

APPELLATION: Columbia Valley
COMPOSITION: 100% Cabernet Franc
MATURATION: Aged 19 months in seasoned French oak barrels
CELLARING: Approachable now, will peak in 4 – 6 years

VISIT OUR STORE

Buy this wine by scanning image on left

TruthTeller Winery WOODINVILLE

Chris and Dawn Loeliger are the first to admit that they created TruthTeller after years of practice drinking wine. It was their last name, Loeliger, that served as the inspiration behind the label, though. It's Swiss and roughly translates to "village jester"—an entertainer who tells the truth through comedy. Humor and honesty; it's a perfect balance—just like their wine.

A joyful sense of fun has always been behind Chris and Dawn's wine journey. They laugh when recalling their much younger days in Dallas, Texas, when they even went so far as to "research" what wines tasted best in their aluminum camping cups. But, what else could one expect from Chris, an aerospace engineer with an entrepreneurial, adventurous heart that took him from Tokyo, to the Peace Corps, to home renovation and real estate, to wine. As for Dawn, her impressive business acumen includes strategy, marketing, sales, consulting, and innovation development.

Talk about a power couple. Now, the winery has become even more of a family affair, with the addition of Dawn's son, Keith, as an assistant winemaker and tasting room manager for the Woodinville location. Even younger brother Andrew gets in on the fun by creating many of the sly wine names that hint at the winery's "jester" roots. However, this family pulls no punches when it comes to the quality of their bottles, including Viognier, Chardonnay, Syrah, Cabernet Sauvignon, and various Bordeaux blends. They know all too well that wine always tells the truth—the truth of the terroir, the stewardship and skill of the vineyard managers, and the craftsmanship of the winemaker.

LEFT Owners, winemakers, business managers, and almost every other job. In this family owned and operated winery, these three do it all.

ABOVE LEFT: TruthTeller's award-winning reserve Cabernet Sauvignon, The Confidante, in the Woodinville tasting room.

ABOVE RIGHT: Bottling day for Quip, TruthTeller's newest offering and their first Rosé.
Photographs by Richard Duval

VISCON CELLARS WEST SEATTLE

At Viscon Cellars, the premise is simple: Owner-winemaker Ben Viscon and his wife, Susan, believe that great wine should be a part of everyday life. It's a passion the couple discovered in the late '90s when they moved to Seattle and fell in love with Washington wines and the diversity of the Pacific Northwest's viniculture.

Once Ben tried his hand at making wine—even attending the University of California, Davis–College of Viticulture and Enology to perfect his knowledge—there was no looking back. His craft has since grown from a small basement hobby to a flourishing boutique winery in urban West Seattle.

What sets Viscon Cellars apart is the locally produced feel of the brand and their wines, with small-lot production that sources fruit from premier Washington grape growers to yield award-winning—yet approachable—wines that are just as delicious when paired with an everyday meal as with a special occasion.

LEFT Winemaker and owner of Viscon Cellars, Ben Viscon, is on hand at the west Seattle tasting room to help you enjoy Viscon Cellars wines.

ABOVE LEFT: Iconic Vine Etched Sign for Viscon Cellars in West Seattle.

ABOVE RIGHT: Viscon Cellars is pouring four to six wines at any time. Customers can sample and buy the wines directly from the tasting room in West Seattle.
Photographs by Richard Duval

The Viscon Cellars portfolio predominantly focuses on Bordeaux varietals including Cabernet Sauvignon, Merlot, Cabernet Franc, and Malbec. Rhône varietals include Syrah and Viognier, and there's also a Chardonnay in the mix.

The Viscons love the community that wine creates, and their warm, mid-century modern winery is a testament to that neighborhood spirit. They feature local artists on rotation every quarter at the winery and also actively participate in the West Seattle Art Walk.

TOP: Viscon Cellars sources several Bordeaux varietals from Kiona Vineyard.

ABOVE: Viscon Cellars sources Cabernet Sauvignon and Syrah grapes from Blue Mountain Vineyard.

RIGHT: Viscon Cellars Winery Tasting Room. Iconic Urban Tasting Room in Urban West Seattle.
Photographs by Richard Duval

PILOT LIGHT

GOURMET PAIRINGS

Pairs well with rich food that
have a touch of spice—such
as a grilled ribeye steak with a
peppercorn demi-glace.

TASTING NOTES

The 2014 Pilot Light has a deep purple color. Aromas of coffee
and mocha give way to tastes of sun-ripened warm blackberries
with a hint of vanilla. Slight tannins lead to a smooth, lingering
warm finish.

WINEMAKER'S INSIGHT

For me, Pilot Light is a name reserved for wines that I am
especially proud of; wines that exemplify the reason I make wine
and want to share it with my friends and neighbors. It's what
keeps me going, and doing what I am doing. The 2014 Pilot
Light is from Kiona Vineyard on Red Mountain and features hand-
picked, partial whole cluster fermentation followed by secondary
fermentation in French oak barrels.

AWARDS & DISTINCTIONS

Gold medal in the Cascadia Wine Competition

TECHNICAL DATA

APPELLATION: Red Mountain
COMPOSITION: 100% Malbec
MATURATION: Aged 36 months in 100% French oak barrels, once used.
CELLARING: Drinks beautifully now and will continue to mature in the
bottle for 15-plus years.

LEARN MORE

Visit our website by scanning the image on the left

CENTRAL WASHINGTON

Presented by The Red Mountain AVA

Cairdeas - Winery, page 129

Photograph courtesy of Red Mountain AVA

Sagemoor, page 191

In the center of the Columbia Valley AVA, distinctive sub-appellations produce some of the finest wine the state has to offer. Whether it's the rich heritage of Red Mountain, the notable reds from Horse Heaven Hills, or any of the numerous sub-appellations in the region, Central Washington has a flavor all its own.

On a southwest-facing slope in south-central Washington, sits Red Mountain AVA, first planted in 1975 but officially founded as an AVA in 2001. Its distinction lies in the fact that it's the smallest and warmest wine grape growing region in the state, at just 4,040 acres. With consistent winds, a gentle south slope, and notable heat profile, the AVA is one of the best places in the nation to grow Cabernet Sauvignon, along with a variety of other wine grapes. The unique flavor profiles captured in Red Mountain wines beckon to first-time vineyard and winery owners. As a result, it is the most densely-planted AVA, with 57 percent of the AVA planted with wine grapes. Red Mountain's distinctive wines warranted its own AVA within the larger Yakima Valley AVA.

Yakima Valley AVA enjoys the status of the state's first federally recognized AVA, established in 1983. More than 60 wineries and over 18,000 vineyard acres call Yakima Valley home. Here, the most widely planted grape is Chardonnay, followed by Merlot and Cabernet Sauvignon. The appellation's diversity yields a broad range of styles, from Pinot Gris, Sauvignon Blanc, and Gewürztraminer to Syrah, Cabernet Franc, and more.

The Columbia River runs alongside Horse Heaven Hills AVA, established in 2005. With approximately 66 percent red varieties and 34 percent white, the AVA has been home to growers since 1972. That first planting is now Champoux Vineyards, one of the most acclaimed vineyards in the state. With 16,070 acres planted to grapes, the AVA represents a quarter of the state's total grape production, primarily Cabernet Sauvignon, Merlot, Chardonnay, Riesling, and Syrah, with 37 total varieties planted in vineyards across the AVA.

14 Hands Winery PROSSER

Named for the unbridled spirit of the wild horses that once roamed eastern Washington, 14 Hands Winery represents the frontier energy of the American West. Measuring just 14 hands high—a traditional metric for determining a horse's height—the region's wild horses thrived in the rugged landscape much like the grapes of 14 Hands wine do today: with tenacity and spirit. Since 2005, 14 Hands has been winning over its fans through its vibrant and approachable wines. In 2014, a dedicated winery and tasting room in Prosser, Washington, was completed to charm guests from all over the world.

Winemaker Keith Kenison has been with 14 Hands since the beginning, crafting world-class wines that are appreciated by fans and acknowledged by top wine publications. Keith's passion for wine is apparent; it's not uncommon to find him walking the vineyards and tasting the fruit. His approach is practical, allowing the fruit to express itself with as few manipulations as possible to preserve the integrity of the product. The goal is to produce wine that pleases the customer first, and the winery has done just that.

14 Hands wines are known for their big, fruit-forward reds and crisp, juicy whites. The portfolio features a wide range of wines that can be enjoyed at any occasion including a reserve tier, red and white blends, and even bubbly. Tastings are available daily at the charmingly rustic tasting room, where the essence of Horse Heaven Hills serves as the backdrop for seasonal events and guest education.

LEFT The 14 Hands tasting room was inspired by the landscape of the Horse Heaven Hills, as well as the history of the region.

ABOVE RIGHT Set in the picturesque Horse Heaven Hills, 14 Hands Winery offers daily tastings of highly-rated wines.
Photographs courtesy of 14 Hands Winery

ALEXANDRIA NICOLE CELLARS PATERSON

For Jarrod and Ali Boyle, founders and owners of Alexandria Nicole Cellars, winemaking has been a grand adventure. A Prosser native, Jarrod developed a deep appreciation for the land after years of vineyard management, part of which included serving as the assistant viticulturist at Hogue Cellars under Dr. Wade Wolfe. Here, Jarrod realized his passion for grape growing and winemaking. Subsequent years of further training at UC Davis, the help of consultants, and tasting as many different wines as he could get his hands on led to Jarrod—along with Ali—planting grapes in 1998.

Alexandria Nicole Cellars, lovingly named for Ali by her husband, sources grapes from its Estate Vineyard, Destiny Ridge. With over 20 varieties planted in their vineyard, they are intent on crafting wines that stylistically speak to the terroir from which the grapes come. Crafting wines that are well-balanced and elegantly approachable.

In the vineyard, Jarrod works alongside a devoted crew to oversee the quality of the fruit that goes into every bottle of Alexandria Nicole Cellars wine that comes from the 267-acre Destiny Ridge Vineyard. Located along the ridge line of Horse Heaven Hills it is overlooking the Columbia River allowing for the maritime influence of the river which imparts conditions similar to that of a coastal region, serving to protect the vines year round. The river never freezes, even on the coldest of days, but produces a fog that blankets the vines and insulates them. Wind from the river keeps the air moving in spring and summer months thus reducing the likelihood of natural enemies to the vines—mildew and fungal disease. Depending on where one stands

FACING PAGE: Located in the Horse Heaven Hills, guests enjoy the Estate Vineyard & Winery Tasting Room.

ABOVE: Jarrod and Ali Boyle enjoying a walk through their estate Destiny Ridge Vineyard.
Photographs courtesy of Alexandria Nicole Cellars

in the vineyard, the soil conditions vary as well. Its five unique topography areas include clay, limestone, schist—medium-sized mineral rocks—and gravel along with sandy topsoils.

These climate and soil conditions make Destiny Ridge a prime location for a multitude of varietals. Here, the Boyles and their team have planted Riesling, Viognier, Sauvignon Blanc, Roussanne, Marsanne, Merlot, Malbec, Tempranillo, Mourvèdre, Syrah, Grenache, Cabernet Sauvignon, Cabernet Franc, and Petit Verdot.

The partnership that Jarrod has with the land includes sustainable vineyard management, which integrates three goals: environmental health, economic profitability, and social and economic equity. Sustainability is the consistent goal for the winery and its team, who take their role in land stewardship seriously. As they have traveled the world and seen what other wineries have done, the Boyles are even more appreciative of the fertile land from which their grapes come. It's simply perfect for wine.

Located among rolling hills, the winery occupies a large red barn. Set among the green of the hills and the vines, the contrast of color is absolutely stunning. Casitas—really, tiny houses—are available for guest lodging and tie in the barn's bold red color.

TOP: Rolling hills of Destiny Ridge Vineyard.

BELOW: Spectaular skies and colors are common place at the Ridgeline Grenache block at Destiny Ridge.
Photographs courtesy of Alexandria Nicole Cellars

DESTINY BORDEAUX RED BLEND

GOURMET PAIRINGS

Pairs well with roast lamb with garlic and rosemary, roast duck, or your favorite grilled meats.

TASTING NOTES

Our Destiny Bordeaux Red Blend represents the best of what Destiny Ridge has to offer. Crafted from all six Bordeaux varietals, the blend is complex and elegant. The palate dances with red and black currant, plum, cassis, olive, and dried herbs with hints of vanilla. Aromas of vanilla, caramel, and mocha complement the palate beautifully. The wine is full-bodied, with an amazing balance of richness, a long finish, and bold tannins that promise longevity.

WINEMAKER'S INSIGHT

Our Destiny Ridge Estate Vineyard overlooks the Columbia River and sits high on the ridge. Here, unique soils impart a distinctive flavor to our Bordeaux varietals. The vineyard is carefully managed throughout the year. At harvest, grapes are hand-harvested and hand-processed to ensure consistent quality in the bottle before aging in French oak barrels for 20 months.

AWARDS AND DISTINCTIONS

93 points – Wine Spectator

TECHNICAL DATA

APPELLATION: Horse Heaven Hills

COMPOSITION: 58% Cabernet Sauvignon, 16% Merlot, 10% Cabernet Franc, 8% Malbec, 6% Petit Verdot, 2% Carménère

MATURATION: Aged 20 months in 100% French Oak

CELLARING: Exceptional now but gains complexity and harmony for five to 10 years

LEARN MORE

Learn more about this wine and our winery by scanning the image on the left

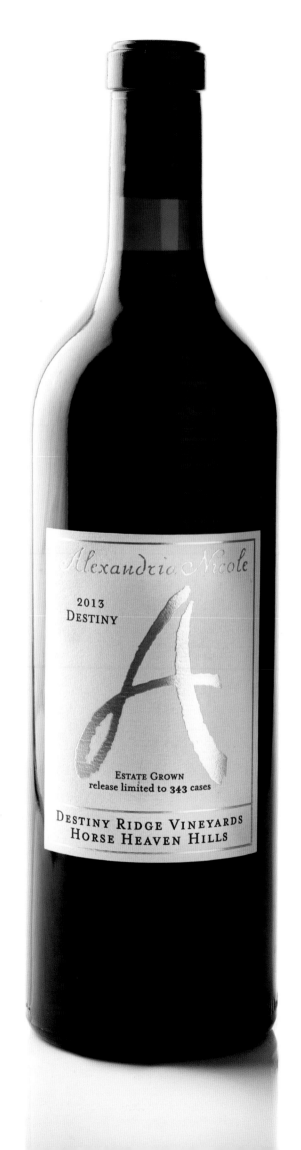

JET BLACK SYRAH

GOURMET PAIRINGS

Pairs well with slow-roasted pork and other hearty meat dishes.

TASTING NOTES

Bold and clean, this energetic Syrah presents a perfumed bouquet that's filled with the sultry aromas of dark cherry, licorice, mocha, and some hints of cracked pepper and herbs. The palate is robust, coating the mouth with thick flavors of blueberry jam, wild vine blackberries, toasted nuts, and an intricate layer of leathery spice. The mid-palate presents a plethora of texture yet manages to stay fresh and graceful with a juicy acidity and elegantly sleek tannins that segue into a luxurious and lengthy finish.

WINEMAKER'S INSIGHT

Our Jet Black Syrah hails from our Destiny Ridge Estate Vineyard. Small individual lots of whole berry fermentation create the deep and intense black color in this special wine. It's energetic and bold. We hand-harvest and hand-process grapes during our passionate winemaking process, to ensure consistency among vintages.

AWARDS AND DISTINCTIONS

91 points – Wine Spectator

TECHNICAL DATA

APPELLATION: Horse Heaven Hills
COMPOSITION: 100% Syrah
MATURATION: Aged 18 months in 35% new French oak and 65% one-year-old French oak barrels
CELLARING: Exceptional now with proper decanting and ages well for three to five years

VISIT OUR STORE

Buy this wine by scanning image on left

TOP & BELOW: The Estate at Destiny Ridge is perched along the ridge line surrounded by stunning views of both the vineyard and the Columbia River.
Photographs courtesy of Alexandria Nicole Cellars

The casitas have a more urban feel, but the Estate House, set on a ridge line above the vines, possesses an Old World elegance. Indeed, one feels as if they are approaching a European villa when it comes into view. The Estate House includes three luxurious guest suites and the Boyles plan to add other amenities to the winery in coming years to create a spectacular destination for tourists and locals alike.

Whether guests visit the winery itself or one of the two tasting rooms located in Prosser and Woodinville, Alexandria Nicole Cellars wines are sure to captivate the palate and delight the

senses. Critically acclaimed locally and nationwide, the wines at Alexandria Nicole Cellars is unlike any other. From the incredible Shepherds Mark Rhone white blend of Viognier with lesser-known Roussanne and Marsanne to the Jet Black Syrah that is, in fact, nearly black in color, there's something special about these wines. Traditional favorites including the Quarry Butte Red Table Wine and Alderdale Cabernet Sauvignon are elegant enough for celebrating milestones and are crafted to cellar well, while some surprises like the Cabernet Franc Rosé can be found for purchase at the winery.

Wine Club members enjoy a discount on all purchases and access to the Members Only Wine Club rooms in both tasting rooms. Behind hidden door, a portfolio of "Members Only" wines are held for this exclusive group. Known for hosting a wide array of unique events for their Wine Club Members, Alexandria Nicole Cellars also enjoys participating in many of the industry favorites such as Taste Washington, Spring Barrel Tasting, Trail Drive, Catch the Crush and Thanksgiving in Wine Country.

As the Boyles continue their pursuit to craft elegantly approachable wine, their passion will surely fuel the winery into the next generation, inspiring wine lovers for decades to come.

TOP: The Boyle Family (from left to right) Matti, Seph, Ali, Jarrod and Kol enjoyiing a stroll through the estate vineyard.
Photograph by Sunny Wright Photography

MIDDLE: The "Jet Black" Tiny House. Alexandria Nicole Cellars has four Tiny Houses located within their Estate vineyard for guests can enjoy a unique and relaxing escape to Wine Country.
Photograph courtesy of Alexandria Nicole Cellars

BOTTOM: Wind Spires were installed as part of Alexandria Nicole Cellars's commitment to be sustainable and environmentally conscious.
Photograph courtesy of Alexandria Nicole Cellars

SHEPHERDS MARK

GOURMET PAIRINGS

Pairs perfectly with rich fish or poultry dishes and heavy cream sauces.

TASTING NOTES

Our Viognier-based blend, Shepherds Mark, presents a beautiful harmony of lavender, herbal tea, honey, and freshly-picked stone fruit, leading to an aromatic profile rich with complexity. A weighty palate of honeysuckle, tangerine, and Meyer lemon are pursued by an enticing flash of acidity that balances out the wine and lends to the sustained and elegant finish.

WINEMAKER'S INSIGHT

The Shepherds Mark Rhone blend of Roussanne, Marsanne, and Viognier is the first to be produced in Washington State and has been our signature white wine since 2004. Named for the early-1900s pioneer sheepherders who left their mark on the Horse Heaven Hills in the form of rock monuments, this monumental wine is crafted from our Destiny Ridge Estate Vineyard grapes. Attentive viticulture management, balanced crop levels, and hand-harvesting and hand-processing make this wine an exceptional example of what Horse Heaven Hills white wines can be.

AWARDS & DISTINCTIONS

90 points – Wine Spectator

TECHNICAL DATA

APPELLATION: Horse Heaven Hills
COMPOSITION: 62% Viognier, 20% Marsanne, 18% Roussanne
MATURATION: Fermented in stainless steel
CELLARING: Excellent now and will age for up to 5 years after vintage

LEARN MORE

Learn more about this wine and our winery by scanning the image on the left

AMBASSADOR WINES BENTON CITY

Founded on the simple belief that the experience of drinking wine is quite unlike any other, Ambassador Wines of Washington began as an idea and has flourished into an award-winning winery with a portfolio of enchanting wines. The founding partners of Ambassador Wines of Washington set out to focus on growing and selling wine grapes from their Red Mountain vineyard. The land was purchased in 2004 and 2005, and yielded its first harvest in 2008. When it became apparent that the 2008 harvest would leave them with an excess of fruit, the partners decided to make wine as well; the first wine from Ambassador Wines of Washington was its 2008 Estate Syrah. The founders like to say they got into the wine business "backward," taking the more expensive and bolder approach to winemaking by buying a world-class stretch of land on Red Mountain and only afterward focusing on bottling wine. By approaching winemaking in this way, the team has been able to control the quality of Ambassador Wines and maintain economically viable, socially supportive, and ecologically sound practices.

Through a dedication to responsible land stewardship, the eclectic team has created a delightful offering of wines including Cabernet Sauvignon, Cabernet Franc, Merlot, Malbec, Petite Verdot, Syrah, and Grenache. Each member lends his or her special skills and diverse background to the success of Ambassador Wines. Vineyard manager, Dick Boushey—who also owns Boushey Vineyards with wife Luanne—serves on the boards of the Washington Wine Commission, the Washington Association of Wine Grape Growers, the Wine Yakima Valley, and other wine-oriented organizations. Winemaker Mike MacMorran put his medical career on hold to pursue his dream of owning a winery and brings

FACING PAGE: Ambassador Vineyard on Red Mountain.
Photograph by Richard Duval

TOP LEFT: Ambassador's Managing Partners (left to right):
Mike Amato, Allison Engman and Michael Towers.
Photograph by Richard Duval

ESTATE GRENACHE

GOURMET PAIRINGS
Exceptionally food-friendly, Estate Grenache pairs beautifully with a variety of cuisines, including roasted meats and roasted vegetables with spices, sage, and rosemary.

TASTING NOTES
With a nice cedar spice, cinnamon, and hints of ripe plum and dark cherry pie, the wine is rich and full, with a bit of spice, cedar, and vanilla that carries into a soft finish.

WINEMAKER'S INSIGHT
Made with 100 percent Red Mountain grapes, the Grenache is a late-ripening red varietal that thrives in Red Mountain AVA's hot climate resulting in grapes with intense flavors and structure.

AWARDS & DISTINCTIONS
91 points – International Wine Report

TECHNICAL DATA

APPELLATION: Red Mountain
COMPOSITION: Primarily Grenache, with Petit Verdot and Syrah (varies by vintage)
MATURATION: Aged 18 months in new and neutral French and American oak, then at least one year in the bottle before release
CELLARING: Delicious now but ages well for up to 10 years

LEARN MORE

Learn more about Ambassador Wines by scanning the image to left his expertise to Ambassador Wines of Washington along with consulting winemaker, Tom Rinaldi. Tom has worked in Napa Valley for over three decades, having built a career on expertly crafting elegant Cabernet Sauvignons and Merlots. Mike Amato, partner, hails from the world of finance and works to develop the marketing and branding strategy for Ambassador Wines of Washington. Like Amato, Allison Engman, partner and Chief Operating Officer, also brings a finance background to the winery, along with experience in event planning with a multitude of charities throughout the Puget Sound area. She manages all facets of the winery business including sales and distribution, as well as marketing, events, and compliance. Engman's father, Michael Towers, brings his production experience to the team, drawing from his past experience with Duckhorn Vineyards in Napa Valley.

Despite coming from rather diverse backgrounds within and beyond the wine industry, the team maintains a great sense of humor about winemaking. In fact, it's one of the three guiding principles at Ambassador Wines of Washington: "Take the process, not ourselves, seriously." The team also believes that life is too short to drink anything other than spectacular wine, and finally, they will only put their names on truly exceptional wine.

ABOVE & LEFT: Ambassador's Woodinville tasting room features a sophisticated ambience that feels miles away from it's industrial warehouse location.
Photographs by Richard Duval

Together, they not only make wonderful wine, but they have fun doing it. That spirit carries over to the winery's Woodinville Tasting Room, located in the Warehouse District. Indoor and outdoor tasting areas offer guests a variety of places to relax and sample available wines Friday through Sunday. The tasting room team is dedicated to creating exceptional experiences for patrons by providing fantastic service and events throughout the year including Corks and Canvas Painting and Wine parties, holiday celebrations, and Off the Vine Comedy nights—just more evidence of the Ambassador Wine team's joie de vivre and love of wine. With outstanding recognition from International Wine Report, Wine Enthusiast, the Seattle Wine Awards, and more, it's clear that Ambassador Wines has found the perfect formula for crafting delightful wine experiences that showcase the region.

ABOVE: The tasting room combines fun, elegance and great wine to create magical experiences for guests.
Photographs by Richard Duval

ESTATE PLENIPOTENTIARY CABERNET SAUVIGNON

GOURMET PAIRINGS

To match the richness and tannic structure of this wine, pair with marinated short ribs, richly-sauced filet mignon, or a juicy, grilled ribeye steak.

TASTING NOTES

Dried figs, plums, blackberry, dark chocolate, with a hint of coconut, and slight coffee and leather flavors mingle in the Estate Plenipotentiary Cabernet Sauvignon. This wine is big, full, and tannic. Its great length lingers on, delighting the palate with blackberry and dark chocolate flavors.

WINEMAKER'S INSIGHT

Made with grapes hailing from the Red Mountain AVA, Washington's warmest growing region with broad, southwest-facing slopes, the wine is full-bodied, dark, and dense, with dark fruit aromas and flavors. It showcases the epitome of what Red Mountain AVA has to offer.

AWARDS & DISTINCTIONS

Awards & Distinctions: 91 points – International Wine Report

TECHNICAL DATA

APPELLATION: Red Mountain
COMPOSITION: : Primarily Cabernet Sauvignon with a blend of Bordeaux varieties depending on vintage
MATURATION: Aged 18 months in new and neutral French and American oak, then at least one year in the bottle before release
CELLARING: Delicious now but has potential for up to 10 years

ORDER OUR WINE

Visit our store and buy Ambassador Wines by scanning image on left.

BARNARD GRIFFIN RICHLAND

Growing up in the San Francisco Bay area and working at his uncle's Napa Valley vineyard nourished an early passion for Barnard Griffin co-owner and winemaker Rob Griffin, who fell in love with the culture and practice of winemaking from an early age. At the University of California, Davis, he earned a Bachelor's degree in Fermentation Science, after which he worked for a few years in Sonoma Valley.

But, in 1977, Rob took a leap of faith and set out to explore unchartered wine territory, traveling to Washington—what was then an emerging viticulture region. In this "wild west" of winemaking, Rob made wine at some of the state's earliest wineries including Preston Wine Cellars and The Hogue Cellars before launching his own label, Barnard Griffin, with wife Deborah Barnard in 1983.

Although they began with little more than a few thousand pounds of borrowed fruit and a rented cellar, Rob and Deborah's winery has now grown to be one of the most celebrated and award-winning in Washington—and Rob has even been called the "dean of winemakers" by The Seattle Times' wine columnist Andy Perdue and is considered the longest practicing winemaker in the state.

In 1996, Rob and Deborah built the permanent home for Barnard Griffin Winery in Richland, where it remains to this day—albeit in quite an expanded form. The beautiful campus includes not only their production facility and tasting room, but also a full-service restaurant that offers lunch and dinner

FACING PAGE: Co-owners Rob Griffin and Deborah Barnard share a barrel sample of an upcoming wine release.
Photograph by Darrin Schreder

ABOVE: The Barnard Griffin family shares a smile, and a glass of wine in the cellar.
Photograph by Richard Breshears Photography

along with a fused glass art studio that hosts classes operated by Deborah, who is an established artist in her own right.

Because of Barnard Griffin's sheer volume and broad distribution, many perceive it to be much larger than it is—when, in fact, it is one of the very few medium-size wineries that remains entirely family owned and operated.

Nearly half of Barnard Griffin's wine production comes from the winery's estate vineyard, Caroway, while the remaining fruit is sourced from some of the best vineyards in Washington's Columbia Valley. As one of the first winemakers in the state, Rob quickly learned how to select the optimal vineyard sites in the region to ensure consistency and high quality. From the first release in 1984, to the winery's current annual production of 70,000 cases, growth has been driven organically by consumer demand.

TOP: Front view of the Barnard Griffin property which includes a tasting room as well as a restaurant and fused glass studio.
Photograph by Richard Duval

BELOW LEFT: The winery hosts "the kitchen at Barnard Griffin" which focuses on being globally influenced and regionally driven.
Photograph by Richard Breshears Photography

BELOW RIGHT: Assistant winemaker, and second generation Megan Hughes walks the block and samples Cabernet grapes straight from the vineyard.
Photograph by Darrin Schreder

COLUMBIA VALLEY CHARDONNAY

GOURMET PAIRINGS
Pairs beautifully with seared Arctic char with Mediterranean potatoes.

TASTING NOTES

Barnard Griffin has produced this elegant and balanced Chardonnay since 1983. Winemaker Rob Griffin favors grapes from six to eight vineyards in this Columbia Valley blend. The 45 percent barrel fermentation adds creaminess to the mid-palate and finish while the 55 percent cool stainless steel fermentation ensures varietal fruitiness and a refreshing acidity. Oak character complements the aromas and flavors—but not at the expense of the true fruit flavors.

WINEMAKER'S INSIGHT

The core of this multi-vineyard blend is our Estate Vineyard located south of Kennewick in Finley, Washington. Wine grapes were first planted on this site in the late 1960s; it's a location of proven quality and is moderately warm, allowing correct maturity in the grapes. When we started producing this wine, barrel fermentation was a new idea in Washington. Now, this Chardonnay has been a regional favorite for more than 35 years.

AWARDS & DISTINCTIONS

33 released vintages with awards and scores too numerous to list.

TECHNICAL DATA

APPELLATION: Columbia Valley
COMPOSITION: 100% Chardonnay
MATURATION: Aged six to eight months in French oak barrels
CELLARING: At its best at about two to three years

LEARN MORE

Learn more about this wine and our winery by scanning the image on the left

CABERNET SAUVIGNON RESERVE

GOURMET PAIRINGS

Our chefs recommend a nicely seared ribeye cap with parsnip puree.

TASTING NOTES

At Barnard Griffin, Reserve wines are carefully selected from the best vineyard sites and the best individual barrels from a given year. Reserve is a word perhaps out of fashion, but it has deep meaning for this pioneering winery.

WINEMAKER'S INSIGHT

A chorus of cherry, orange zest, and toasty vanilla oak flavors greets the palate. The wine displays a very ripe and dense character which is nicely offset by juicy acidity. Serve this stately, well-structured Cabernet Sauvignon with hearty meats and other dishes that call for a rich, full-bodied red.

AWARDS AND DISTINCTIONS

93 points, Wine Spectator
Stan Clarke Award for Best Cabernet Sauvignon in Washington

TECHNICAL DATA

APPELLATION: Columbia Valley
COMPOSITION: Cabernet Sauvignon with small amounts of Petit Verdot and Merlot for balance.
MATURATION: Aged 18 to 24 months in French oak barrels.
CELLARING: These are long-lived wines which reward aging for at least 15 years. It is balanced at release, but cellar worthy.

VISIT OUR STORE

Buy this wine by scanning image on left

Barnard Griffin produces a wide range of popular varietals including Chardonnay, Cabernet, Merlot, and Sauvignon Blanc. Visitors to the winery are also offered the exclusive range of limited production and reserve wines available only at the winery.

Rob's early vision of handcrafting the highest quality Washington wine and his uncompromising attention to quality, consistency, and character continue to be the driving forces at Barnard Griffin—especially as he and Deborah move to incorporate a second generation of leadership into their winemaking family. Their daughter, Megan Hughes, who likewise developed a passion for Washington wine from an early age, acts as assistant winemaker and enologist, thus following in her pioneering father's trailblazing footsteps.

TOP: The kitchen at Barnard Griffin includes a stunning glass bar made by co-owner Deborah Barnard and is open for lunch and dinner most days.
Photograph by Richard Breshears Photography

BELOW: The tasting room is open daily and includes a comfortable atmosphere to mingle and appreciate the wines created here.
Photograph by Richard Breshears Photography

BOUDREAUX CELLARS

Years of appreciating fine wines, identifying the oldest, highest quality, and most complex blocks of Cabernet Sauvignon, and learning from some of the greatest winemakers in the world have culminated in Boudreaux Cellars, a winery that epitomizes the value of playing the long game in the wine industry. What started off as friendly banter one summer evening between owner Rob Newsom and winemaker Gary Figgins—"Well, why don't you just make your own wine?" Gary half-joked when Rob complained about the price of some wines—has become a boutique winery that marries a sense of humor with very serious winemaking.

Boudreaux wines are smooth, deep, layered, flowered, and offer mysterious nuances of smoke, hickory, oak, cherry, blackberry, and candy. Insight from master winemakers Gary and Chris Figgins from Leonetti Cellars, John Abbot from Devona Winery in Walla Walla, and others inspired Rob Newsom's path from wine lover to winemaker. Since 1998, when Rob began making homemade wine, he has appreciated the time it takes to craft truly captivating wine. In 2001, his first commercial wines were produced, and Chris Figgins recommended Rob name his wines Boudreaux, after the infamous Cajun folklore character Rob told stories about when he first met the Figginses. The name stuck, and the winery was born.

FACING PAGE: Boudreaux Cellars is nestled in an inspiring setting in Icicle Canyon.
Photograph by Rob Newsom

ABOVE: Winemaker Rob Newsom inspects the 35-year old Cabernet vines at Bacchus Vineyard Block Nine.
Photograph by Keely Newsom

A combination of art and science, winemaking at Boudreaux Cellars is meticulous but also infused with Rob's sense of humor. He often crafts ditties for each one: "Drink this Merlot, eat smoked Coho, kick off your flip-flops, dance on rooftops."

Rob's daughter with wife Tamara, Keely Newsom, assists Rob in the winery. Having grown up around the cellars and wine presses, Keely learned how important generational winemaking is from Gary Figgins and today ensures that Boudreaux wines will endure for generations to come.

Located four miles off the power grid, Boudreaux Cellars is the only Washington winery that's 100 percent self-powered. Here, nature plays an integral role in the winemaking process. The 200-barrel cellar is housed completely underground and allows for consistent cool temperatures and an extended barreling period of two to three years—giving the wine extra time to rest before bottling. Gravity transports wines from the press to the barrel, and the entire process combines modern technology with Old-World tried-and-true techniques.

When guests arrive at the winery on Icicle Road, they're greeted by the local granite stone façade of the winery. Majestic trees and spectacular views make visiting the winery's tasting room a destination worth experiencing. Boudreaux Cellars is open by appointment only, though, so visitors are encouraged to plan ahead. At the Boudreaux Tasting Room in Leavenworth, though, no appointment is needed. Guests can enjoy a little piece of the French Quarter at the Leavenworth tasting room, where gaslights, a zinc-topped bar, and big bottles of Boudreaux wines provide ambiance and a chance to sample Boudreaux Cellars' award-winning wines.

TOP LEFT: Caylan Haehl racking wines and cleaning barrels on the crush pad at Boudreaux Cellars
Photograph by Rob Newsom

BELOW LEFT: Our all female bottling team handles the bottling line at the winery.
Photograph by Stacia Lee

ABOVE: Winemakers Rob and Keely Newsom, daddy/daughter at the end of Crush 2017.
Photograph by Audre' Kelley

CABERNET SAUVIGNON RESERVE

GOURMET PAIRINGS
Pairs well with speck-wrapped filet mignon grilled over applewood with baked sweet potato, pan-fried okra, butter lettuce salad.

TASTING NOTES
Our high-toned, smoky Cabernet Sauvignon Reserve will make you smile as its flavors of toasted pecan, molasses, and cassis with dried cherries and violets dance in your mouth. Reminiscent of giant, smooth Old-World Cabernet Sauvignon, this wine gives a lasting finish and will delight you again and again.

WINEMAKER'S INSIGHT
Seventy-five percent of our Cabernet Sauvignon Reserve is composed of fruit from the Champoux Vineyard and 25% from the Leonetti Estate Loess Vineyard.

AWARDS AND DISTINCTIONS
Boudreaux Reserve Cabernets have received ratings from 91-98 points for fifteen vintages. Outstanding vintages include 2003, 2005, 2009, 2012

TECHNICAL DATA

APPELLATION: Washington State
COMPOSITION: 100% Cabernet Sauvignon
MATURATION: Aged 36 months in new French oak
CELLARING: Enjoy upon release; cellars well for up to 20 years

LEARN MORE

Visit our website by scanning the image to left

BOUSHEY VINEYARDS GRANDVIEW

Winemakers and grape-growers have a symbiotic relationship, and Boushey Vineyards is a prime example of this give and take. Set on the southern slopes of the Rattlesnake Mountains, the vineyards are comprised of several sites in a two-mile area in the Yakima Valley. The humble acreage provides 23 varietals, including Syrah, Cabernet Franc, Sangiovese, Merlot, Sauvignon Blanc, and Cabernet Sauvignon.

Richard Boushey first planted vines in 1980, and today the crops produce fruit for a number of Washington wineries, including Almquist, aMaurice, Ambassador, Aniche Cellars; Avennia, Barrage Cellars, Betz Family, Burnt Bridge, Buty, Cairdeas, Callan Cellars, Cavatappi, Chinook, Covington Cellars, Columbia Crest, Damsel Cellars, DeLille Cellars, EFESTE Winery, Eight Bells, Fidelitas Forgeron Cellars, Gamache, Gorman, JM Cellars, K Vintners, Kevin White, Long Shadows, Matthews Cellars, Ott & Murphy, Savage Grace, Sparkman Cellars, Steven, Structure, Swiftwater Cellars, Syncline, Telaya, Tenor, Upchurch, VaPiano, WIT Cellars, and WT Vintners.

The winemakers in turn, have brought out the best of the vineyards' grapes, and rely on the crops year after year. Over time, Boushey has made a great deal of long-term relationships, but is particularly excited to work with new, young winemakers, and watch them flourish.

FACING PAGE: View of Mt. Adams from the top of Boushey Vineyards at 1,375 feet.
Photograph by Andrea Johnson

TOP LEFT: Dick, Luanne and Cooper on the back porch at Boushey Vineyards.
Photograph by Andrea Johnson

TOP RIGHT: Cabernet Sauvignon grapes right before harvest.
Photograph by Richard Duval

RED MOUNTAIN AVA

When Richard Boushey's loyal winemakers asked him to start growing in the Red Mountain AVA, he obliged, and the 38-year industry veteran has learned a few new tricks since he began working there. A steward of the land with a no-shortcut approach, Richard manages vineyards for a number of wineries: Cadence, Ste. Michelle/Antinori, DeLille Cellars, Duckhorn, Efeste, Fidelitas, Hamilton Cellars, Ambassador, and Upchurch. The land produces the highest quality fruit and the best Cabernet in the state, and consequently has attracted winemakers and vineyard owners from around the world. Roughly 75 to 80 percent of the vines in Red Mountain Vineyards are Cabernet Sauvignon vines.

As head of the Washington State Research Committee and member of the Wine Commission Board, Richard believes that Red Mountain Vineyards is one of the key growing areas keeping the state competitive in the premium wine game. It's well-known, attracts visitors from around the world, and consistently produces fruit that winemakers clamor for.

The unique high-tier area sits just west of the Tri-Cities on the east end of Yakima Valley and has maintained a prestigious reputation since its first planting in 1975. Red Mountain is the smallest AVAs in Washington State at only 2,700 plantable acres. It's made up of a tight-knit membership community with its own wine alliance and is managed in a way that aims to keep winemakers happy.

FACING PAGE TOP LEFT: Rainbow over Shaw Vineyards Red Mountain.

FACING PAGE TOP RIGHT: View overlooking Red Mountain and iconic Col Solare winery.

LEFT: View looking east at Red Mountain AVA and the Yakima River.

ABOVE LEFT: Standing on Red Mountain overlooking the vineyards and the Horse Heaven Hills.

ABOVE RIGHT: Harvesting Cabernet for EFESTE Winery at Angela Vineyard.
Photographs by Andrea Johnson

THE BUNNELL FAMILY CELLAR PROSSER

The art of small-lot winemaking is not lost on the team at the Bunnell Family Cellar. Since their first vintage in 2004, the family has made all wines themselves, in one-ton fermentation bins, using a gentle, manual punch-down method. Every decision—from pick, to press, to blending—is made by winemaker Ron Bunnell and his wife and culinary partner, Susan Bunnell. Their philosophy is that nothing replaces the human palate. Lab analysis is important, but it should never supplant the winemaker's personal sensory evaluation, knowledge, and understanding.

A career spanning 35 years has shown Ron the importance of being a good steward of the wine and letting it speak for itself. At their home on the banks of the Yakima River, the Bunnells craft a wide range of small-lot varietal wines and blends. More than two dozen current releases include five different vineyard designated Syrahs and four vineyard designated Cabernets. They regularly produce Grenache, Mourvedre, Petit Verdot, Malbec, Merlot, Sangiovese, Pinot Gris, and Gewürztraminer. Occasionally they craft micro-lots of less than 100 cases of varietals such as Petite Sirah, Counoise, Aglianico, Tempranillo, Dolcetto, and Aligote. Ron specializes in combining flavors, and believes strongly in the inherent advantages of blending. Synergy can be as serendipitous in winemaking as it is in life.

Sample and savor the Bunnell Family's best at one of two locations: Wine o'Clock Wine Bar & Bistro or the Bunnell-Newhouse Tasting Studio. With fine wine and delicious food, the sum is so much greater than its parts. This perfect marriage is exemplified at Wine o'Clock Wine Bar & Bistro; a unique

FACING PAGE Spring at the Bunnell Family Prosser tasting room, Wine o'Clock. When the daffodils come out, al fresco enjoyment can't be far behind.
Photograph by Susan Bunnell

ABOVE LEFT: Danielle pouring wine for a wine club event at the tasting room in Woodinville.
Photograph by Susan Bunnell

ABOVE RIGHT: Ron and Susan Bunnell with a dizzying array of current releases. Select from these, or peruse an extensive wine list going back to 2004.
Photograph by Colby Kuschatka

spot for civilized wining and dining. Guests explore wine flights for the best variety in pairing and sharing, and can sample a new menu of handcrafted dishes created each week in the display kitchen. During summer the herb garden provides a beautiful background for dining al fresco. A little more laid back, the Bunnell-Newhouse Tasting Studio invites you to pull up a barstool and prepare for some serious wine tasting. It's located in the Woodinville wine warehouse district and like the wine bar, showcases wines made by Ron Bunnell for both the Bunnell Family labels and Newhouse Family Vineyards. The tasting selections at both locations change monthly.

Wine flights at Bunnell's tasting rooms and bistro feature primarily vineyard designated wines that show off Washington's dynamic terroir. At Wine o'Clock, half a dozen curated flights comprise the ever-changing offerings, including "Surfeit of Syrahs" and "Game of Rhônes." Visitors experience the differences created by the diverse microclimates and AVAs of Washington State. It's always fun, and always flavorful. Oenophiles can take a trip back in time, thanks to a Coravin system which offers access to an extensive library dating back to 2004. This allows tasters to explore how the wines from the Bunnell Family change and develop over time.

ABOVE: The north-facing slope of the Horse Heaven Hills, home of Discovery Vineyard, with a cascading morning mist.
Photograph by Susan Bunnell

RIGHT: Wining and dining at its finest. The Bunnell Family serves their award winning wines at Wine o'Clock Wine Bar and Bistro.
Photograph by Richard Duval

THE BUNNELL FAMILY CELLAR SYRAH FROM DISCOVERY VINEYARD

GOURMET PAIRINGS

The vibrant black fruit and depth of flavor in this powerful wine make it a natural pairing with a dry-aged ribeye steak, charred rare on the barbeque accented by a green peppercorn compound butter and earthy truffled potatoes.

TASTING NOTES

Characterized by a deep ruby color with substantial density, and blackberry and black cherry fruit aromas with a slight earthiness, fine, soft tannins belie the intensity and power of this wine. The lingering finish has a hint of toast.

WINEMAKER'S INSIGHT

We have worked with the Syrah from Discovery Vineyard since the first crop and have learned how to optimize the fermentation for this exceptional fruit. Hand-picked fruit is destemmed and crushed directly to one-ton fermenters. The crushed grapes are allowed to cold soak for 48 hours, during which time saignée is performed, removing 5-10 percent of the juice from the fermenter to increase the intensity of the finished wine. After the cold soak, the must is inoculated with yeast and punched down 4-5 times daily until approximately 8 brix, then twice daily until press. We will typically press at 3 brix and allow the fermentation to finish in the settling tank or in barrels. After primary fermentation is complete, the wine is inoculated for malo-lactic fermentation.

AWARDS & DISTINCTIONS

Gold at 2017 SF Chronicle Competition
Double Platinum WPNW 2016 Best of the Best
Seattle Metropolitan Magazine top 10 Syrahs
Wine Spectator—94 points
Wine Enthusiast—91 points
Wine Advocate—90 points

TECHNICAL DATA

APPELLATION: Horse Heaven Hills
COMPOSITION: 100% Syrah
MATURATION: Aged 20 months in French and American oak, 25% new.
CELLARING: Drinks beautifully now but will benefit from additional cellaring of a decade or more.

LEARN MORE

Visit our website by scanning the image on the left

CAIRDEAS WINERY LAKE CHELAN

Cairdeas (pronounced "card-is") is an Irish-Gaelic word meaning "friendship, goodwill, or alliance." At Cairdeas Winery, they believe in all three: Good wine should be shared with friends; goodwill should be spread at every opportunity; and alliances should be created with those who share the same passions.

The word also holds special personal meaning for the winery's founders Lacey and Charlie Lybecker, as they especially value the alliance they have made with each other and with those in the industry as well as all the friendships established along the way. What's more, the winery's logo also incorporates the ancient Gaelic Ogham alphabet character of the word "cairdeas," which was illustrated in a relic that Lacey took home from a trip to Ireland with her mom.

As luck would have it, Charlie actually has Lacey to thank for truly igniting his passion for wine. She went on her first wine tasting tour when she was just 19—in Australia, no less—and quickly sought out the wine scene when she moved to Seattle after college graduation. Romantic wine tastings in Woodinville and south Seattle became a regular date activity for the couple. As sparks flew between the two of them, Charlie likewise kindled his love of discovering new bottles. His curiosity piqued, he soon set out to learn what makes a great wine and why the juice turns out the way it does—delving into everything from the vineyard and the barrel, to the yeast and winemaking techniques.

FACING PAGE: Charlie and Lacey Lybecker pose for a photo inside their barrel room, which currently houses 200 barrels of wine.
Photograph by Dalisa Jo Photography

TOP: Freshly harvested Boushey Vineyard Grenache Blanc waiting to go into the press, with the tasting room entrance in the backdrop.
Photograph by Lacey Lybecker

The Lybeckers launched their boutique artisan winery in 2009, and while it was founded in West Seattle, the beautiful wine country in the Lake Chelan Valley eventually called their hearts to that area. In the summer of 2012, they made the move—and their Lake Chelan winery dreams came true. Now, it's the place the couple truly feels at home, together with their two young sons—Eugene and Francis—affectionately referred to as the "whinemakers" of the house. Tannin, the resident wine dog, is also a big part of the family and serves on the greeting committee at Cairdeas.

They've since planted a small estate vineyard featuring head-trained Joseph Phelps clone Syrah and two rare white Rhône varietals. Cairdeas is the first vineyard in the state to plant Picardan, and the second vineyard to plant Clairette Blanche—two varietals that are widely planted in the southern Rhône Valley of France.

ABOVE LEFT: Tasting Room Manager, Danielle, pours Late Harvest Roussanne for winery guests.
Photograph by Richard Duval

ABOVE RIGHT: The tasting room patio is an inviting space for guests to hang out by the fire and enjoy views of the vineyard and the lake.
Photograph by Lacey Lybecker

BELOW LEFT: Winemaker Charlie Lybecker stands outside the Barrel Room on a freshly cleaned crush pad.
Photograph by Dalisa Jo Photography

BELOW RIGHT: Grandma Nellie, the namesake behind signature wine Nellie Mae, joins her grandson Charlie on the crush pad during harvest.
Photograph by Lacey Lybecker

NELLIE MAE

GOURMET PAIRINGS

Spaghetti and clams paired with the white wines of the Cinque Terre was the food highlight of Lacey and Charlie's honeymoon. Their recreation features Nellie Mae in the dish's white wine and herb tomato sauce.

TASTING NOTES

Nellie Mae blends Viognier together with Roussanne. The Viognier contributes floral aromas while the Roussanne gives the wine a creamy mouthfeel. Notes of pineapple and citrus linger on the palate. Nellie is their grandma and Mae crosses both families to represent some of the strongest and most passionate women they know. It pairs beautifully with soft cheese, seafood pasta, and citrus chicken.

WINEMAKER'S INSIGHT

We typically pick both varieties around 24 brix for the flavor profile we are trying to achieve. The grapes are whole cluster pressed and cold settled for 24 to 48 hours. The lots are fermented separately in stainless steel tanks at 55 degrees for about 30 days. We do thorough blending trials to get the best aromatics of Viognier and the texture of Roussanne. The wines are racked at blending and filtered at bottling.

AWARDS & DISTINCTIONS

90 points–Wine Spectator
90 points–Jeb Dunnuck
Seattle Metropolitan Top 25 Wine Under $25

TECHNICAL DATA

APPELLATION: Columbia Valley
COMPOSITION: 70% Viognier, 30% Roussanne
MATURATION: Aged 30 days in stainless steel tanks.
CELLARING: Drink now to enjoy the bright acidity, but age for up to five years to enjoy a richer, creamier texture and deeper tropical fruit notes.

LEARN MORE

Learn more about this wine and our winery by scanning the image on the left

TRÍ

GOURMET PAIRINGS

Chef Aaron Tekulve of Surrell created this smoky beef short rib to play with the Tri's lingering spice. Mushrooms and cabbage in a rosemary Worcestershire sauce take the supporting role to pull all of the flavors together.

TASTING NOTES

Trí, also the Gaelic word for "three," is a blend of three classic southern Rhône varietals. This wine features plum, espresso, and tobacco leaf on the nose with rich notes of fig and white pepper on the palate. It also pairs well with Manchego cheese and lamb burgers.

WINEMAKER'S INSIGHT

The Syrah is whole cluster fermented, no destemming or crushing, stems and all to build body and tannins without the use of new oak. The Grenache and Mourvèdre are both destemmed only—no crushing—to enhance the fruit of the Grenache and the earth and spice of the Mourvèdre. All wines are aged in neutral French oak puncheon to let the varietal characteristics shine through.

AWARDS AND DISTINCTIONS

91 points–Wine Enthusiast
93 points–Jeb Dunnuck
Best of Show Tri Cities Wine Festival
Outstanding! Great Northwest Wine

TECHNICAL DATA

APPELLATION: Yakima Valley
COMPOSITION: 64% Syrah, 24% Mourvèdre, 12% Grenache
MATURATION: Aged in 500-liter neutral French oak puncheon.
CELLARING: Delicious now, but can be cellared for up to 10 years.

VISIT OUR STORE

Buy this wine by scanning image on left

In fact, Lacey and Charlie glean their inspiration from France's prized Rhône region, working exclusively with Rhône varietals to craft both traditional and progressive blends including reds from Syrah, Grenache, Mourvèdre, Counoise, and Cinsault grapes and whites from Viognier, Roussanne, Marsanne, Grenache Blanc, and Picpoul grapes.

They believe Washington provides the opportunity for ultra-premium grape-growing conditions. In addition to their own estate vineyard, they carefully select other vineyards based on location, climate, and soil types that are best suited for each of the grape varietals. Each of their vineyard rows is farmed to exact specifications, so that they can control the quality.

Because every growing region has its own unique characteristics, Lacey and Charlie source fruit from all over the state. This level of variety garners many different flavor profiles while allowing for a true tailoring of the wines to precisely what they have envisioned. At the end of the day, it's all about creating memorable wines that they are proud to call Cairdeas—and to share with friends, naturally!

TOP: Lake Chelan and the Cascade Mountains create a stunning backdrop for Cairdeas Winery's block of Clairette Blanche.
Photograph by Lacey Lybecker

BELOW: Whinemakers Francis and Eugene inspect tiny clusters of Clairette at fruit set.
Photograph by Lacey Lybecker

133

CASCADE CLIFFS VINEYARD & WINERY WISHRAM

At Cascade Cliffs Vineyard & Winery, the philosophy is simple: a profound respect for nature will produce equally profound wines. Owner Robert "Bob" Lorkowski believes in the minimal sculpting of fruit to produce wines that represent the best of what each varietal naturally has to offer. To say that his passion for wine runs in the family is an understatement. From as early as he can remember, Bob would help his parents fill the backseat of the family car with fruit from the local farmers' market and so they could make wine at home. His grandfather was a moonshiner and helped further cultivate Bob's fascination with fermentation. Then as a young man, Bob trained at UC Davis and honed his winemaking skills working for Cavatappi Winery in Kirkland, and Chinook Wines in Prosser.

In the 1990s, while purchasing grapes for his own label, Sha Toe Du Bob, the previous owner of Cascade Cliffs, Ken Adcock, asked Bob if he'd consider taking a permanent interest in the winery, which was established in 1986 with five acres. Bob jumped at the chance and in 1997 purchased the winery and planted an additional 15 acres of grapevines. Since then, Bob has been directly involved with growing grapes and winemaking. His passion is for Piedmont varietals including Barbera, Dolcetto, and Nebbiolo, but Cascade Cliffs Vineyard & Winery also produces Sangiovese, Tempranillo, Cabernet Sauvignon, Merlot, and various blends.

At Bob's side is Vineyard Manager, Assistant Winemaker, and "Jack of all Trades," Edwardo Ornelas. With over 20 years of grape growing experience, Edwardo has been with Cascade Cliffs since inception.

FACING PAGE: So it's said; "If there's water to the left, there's wine to the right." Looking over our Merlot vines into the Cabernet Sauvignon with the Columbia River in the background.

TOP LEFT: The Missoula Floods carved out the Columbia Gorge to create some of the most breath-taking views. This beautiful family and vineyard are framed by basalt cliffs, Horsethief Butte and Mount Hood.
Photographs by Andrea Johnson

ESTATE BARBERA

GOURMET PAIRINGS

Barbera pairs beautifully with a hearty pasta dish with a rich, red sauce or, for a small bite option, a gorgonzola or bleu cheese spread on a baguette.

TASTING NOTES

The high acidity of our Estate Barbera lends itself to a wide variety of food pairings, while its lower tannins allow it to be enjoyed more in its youth than other red wines.

WINEMAKER'S INSIGHT

We have had Barbera plantings on our vineyard since 1990, and some of those are the very first in the Pacific Northwest. The fruit's high acidity, low tannins, and dark pigments make it approachable for novice wine drinkers and connoisseurs alike.

AWARDS & DISTINCTIONS

Gold, Double Gold, Platinum, Best of Best, and Top 100 Wines of Washington

TECHNICAL DATA

APPELLATION: Columbia Valley

COMPOSITION: 100% Barbera

MATURATION: Aged 12 months in American oak.

CELLARING: Delicious upon release and ages well for five to eight years

LEARN MORE

Learn more about our wines and winery by scanning the image on the left or visiting www.cascadecliffs.com

He helped plant the original vines and knows the terroir like the back of his hand. He and Bob have also perfected the punch-down techniques that create consistently delicious Cascade Cliffs wines. General Manager Jared Germain has worked in a variety of positions in the wine industry: wine steward, sommelier, writer, blogger, educator, and his personal favorite, "Cork Dork." His certifications with The Court of Master Sommeliers and The Society of Wine Educators, as well as his extensive travels, help educate visitors on the ins and outs of the wine industry.

Not only does Cascade Cliffs boast three tasting rooms—one at the winery in Wishram, another in Hood River, Oregon, and a third in Woodinville, Washington—but the winery also offers different wine clubs to suit discerning tastes. The Piedmont Club showcases Bob's affinity for the Piedmont varietals Barbera, Dolcetto, and Nebbiolo. These varietals set Cascade Cliffs apart from most producers in the United States and as one of the very first vineyards in the Pacific Northwest to grow these varietals, Cascade Cliffs offers its Piedmont Club members an exclusive opportunity to enjoy these wines-considered to be among the Best of the Best.

The Barbera Club focuses exclusively on the winery's superstar wine: Barbera. Barbera Club members receive a mixed case of new release Barbera wines in the spring and a six pack of

TOP: Our Cabernet Sauvignon vines just before harvest with Horsethief Butte and Mt. Hood in the background.
Photograph by Jared Germain

RIGHT: Our entrance sign created by local talents showcasing massive timbers and iron that is used throughout our winery.
Photograph by James McNamee

the Reserve Barbera wines in the fall. Fans of the winery can also join the Cliff Club, where members receive six bottles of wine four times a year from current and library selections. No matter the club, all members become a "part of the family." This means that they never pay for a wine tasting and can attend specially themed tastings at the winery for free. The team also makes a special effort to get to know each member, providing exclusive access to the winery during visits.

Whether that visit is at the winery in Wishram, or one of the two tasting rooms in the region, guests are continually blown away by the quality of Cascade Cliffs wines. The critics agree: Cascade Cliffs' bottlings have received numerous accolades including being named to the Top 100 Wines by Great Northwest Wine, and multiple Gold, Double Gold, and Platinum awards.

TOP: A view looking northwest through the vineyard toward the cliffs. No matter the season our vineyard is one that is most photographed.
Photograph by Jared Germain

BELOW LEFT: Northwest Wine Summit, Cascadia Wine Competition, and Great Northwest Wine Competition share our love of wine. varietals.
Photograph by James McNamee

BELOW RIGHT: A peek into our barrel room with our current selection of Piedmont varietals.
Photograph by James McNamee

RESERVE ESTATE NEBBIOLO

GOURMET PAIRINGS

Nebbiolo begs for food. Our favorite is to pair it with an earthy mushroom risotto.

TASTING NOTES

At once delicate and intense, our Reserve Estate Nebbiolo is a more traditional, rustic style. Like most Italian wines, it pairs well with a fine meal, but this intense wine can be too much for delicate dishes.

WINEMAKER'S INSIGHT

Nebbiolo is the "headache grape," not because it gives you a hangover, but because it's very difficult to grow. With more leaves and growth than other plants, the vines require an exceptionally high canopy. They also produce the least amount of fruit and have the longest growing season of any of our grapes. Nebbiolo is the first to bud and the last to harvest. The wine ages very well and for much longer than most want to wait to enjoy it.

AWARDS & DISTINCTIONS

Gold, Double Gold, Best in Category, as well as a top pick from Tasting Room Magazine.

TECHNICAL DATA

APPELLATION: Columbia Valley
COMPOSITION: 100% Nebbiolo
MATURATION: Aged 20 months in American oak
CELLARING: Enjoy now or cellar for up to 10 years

ORDER OUR WINE

Visit our wine store by scanning the image to left

CAVE B ESTATE WINERY QUINCY

When he was a young boy growing up in the hustle and bustle of Brooklyn, New York, Vince Bryan, owner of Cave B Estate Winery, used to gaze out at his cheese box window sill radish plantings and dream of wider spaces. Co-owner Carol Bryan spent her childhood summers on the Indiana dunes learning how to be resilient, tenacious, and courageous. As fate would have it, the pair of kindred spirits met in high school and fell in love. After college, they moved, as a young married couple, from Illinois to California, UCLA, from where Vince, a resident in neurosurgery, was called into the Navy during the Vietnam War, ultimately being stationed at the Bremerton Naval Hospital. Little did they know, the assignment would introduce them to their next great love: Washington State, where they eventually settled and raised their family of four children. As a neurosurgeon, Vince experienced the stress of life-and-death scenarios regularly and yearned for a creative project he could share with Carol and their kids. His childhood dreams of becoming a farmer resurfaced, and he and Carol began looking for the perfect spot to grow grapes. It took them about a year of searching, but in 1979, they settled on 260 acres of alfalfa fields and a 50-acre sagebrush field—the home of their future wineries.

The pair planted their first harvest in 1980 and, in 1984, partnered with others to create their first winery, Champs de Brionne. As part of the grand opening, the Bryans built a stage for musical performances. Old irrigation ditches became terraces for people to picnic on, and guests loved the experience so much that the Bryans expanded the Champs de Brionne Summer Music Theater every summer. It eventually became the world-famous Gorge

FACING PAGE: Winemaker Alfredo "Freddy" Arredondo and his two Cellarmasters make a dynamic team turning our 100 percent estate grown grapes into award winning wines.
Photograph by Steve Lentz

ABOVE: The beauty at Cave B Estate Winery is awe inspiring.
Photograph by Carrie Arredondo

Amphitheater, which the couple sold 10 years later—along with the winery building—to MCA Concerts to return their focus to growing exceptional wine grapes.

Another decade later, in 2000, Cave B Estate Winery was established. Named for the historical use of wine caves and the idea that Cave B hopes guests can "B" inspired by the natural beauty, a wide range of events, and the incredible flavor profile of their wines from their all estate vineyards. The winery sits on the original 310-acre property purchased in 1979. Today 17 vineyards, many trees, flowers, and grass grow on the land that possesses so much natural beauty that it takes one's breath away.

The facilities at the winery complement the stunning natural landscape with the original production facility faced, by hand, with rocks from two quarries on the property. A barrel cave was also added at the time, and in 2005, the Bryans built the Cave B Resort, now the Cave B Inn & Spa Resort—that included

TOP: Flower lined walkway to our Quincy tasting room

BE;OW LEFT: Our grape lined Piazza provides a beautiful space for weddings, winemaker dinners and picnics.

BELOW RIGHT: Summer of 2017 marked the debut of our Cave B Summer Music Theater with a concert series from the Yakima Symphony Orchestra. More to come!
Photographs by Carrie Arredondo

MALBEC

GOURMET PAIRINGS

This wine does tremendously well with a wide range of foods. Some of our favorite pairings are roasted squab with huckleberry compote or grilled pork ribs with a blackberry chipotle glaze.

TASTING NOTES

Our Malbec is a generous mouthful of a wine. It offers aromas of dark cherries, wild huckleberries, and blackberries with spicy aromas of cracked black pepper, leather, and tobacco leaf notes and hints of white pepper. The palate is supple with beautifully integrated tannins and food-friendly acidity to make this wine a gem on the dinner table.

WINEMAKER'S INSIGHT

Our Malbec vineyards are planted in well-drained silt/sandy loam soil allowing us to control canopy growth and vine vigor through drip irrigation so that the vines can focus on ripening fruit. Our Malbec is most definitely a robust representation of this variety. It is much bigger in character and complexity than some of its counterparts from Argentina that gave this grape varietal prominence. This wine is fermented in one-ton open top bins and is on the skins for 15+ days to give the wine a deep, inky color.

AWARDS & DISTINCTIONS

Gold Medal – Seattle Wine Awards

TECHNICAL DATA

APPELLATION: Ancient Lakes of Columbia Valley
COMPOSITION: 100% Malbec
MATURATION: Aged 22 months in 225-liter French and American oak
CELLARING: Drinks beautifully upon release but will age well for 10+ years

LEARN MORE

Learn more about this wine and our winery by scanning the image on the left

SAUVIGNON BLANC

GOURMET PAIRINGS

This wine is amazing served alongside fresh oysters on the half shell with a light mignonette. Some favorites are Quilcene, Kumamoto, and Shigoku oysters sourced from Puget Sound.

TASTING NOTES

Our Sauvignon Blanc shows a beautifully distinct varietal character with citrus notes of Meyer lemon and pink grapefruit, perfectly complemented with hints of fresh cut grass, and whispers of boxwood. The natural acidity is harmoniously balanced and complements the flavors encountered on the palate and ending with a fresh, crisp, and clean finish.

WINEMAKER'S INSIGHT

Our Sauvignon Blanc is comprised of three different Estate vineyard blocks, each block giving the wine its own unique character. These blocks have slightly different soil compositions with varying amounts of calcium carbonate, and volcanic derived, basalt rock in the sandy loam soil mixture. The wine is fermented very slowly at cool temperatures with the average alcoholic fermentation taking 30 to 45 days. After fermentation, the wine remains on the lees for added mouthfeel and complexity on the palate.

AWARDS AND DISTINCTIONS

Gold Medal – Seattle Wine Awards

TECHNICAL DATA

APPELLATION: Ancient Lakes of Columbia Valley
COMPOSITION: 95% Sauvignon Blanc, 5% Semillon
MATURATION: 5 months in stainless steel tanks
CELLARING: Brilliant upon release

VISIT OUR STORE

Buy this wine by scanning image on left

the Inn and Tendrils restaurant. The Round House followed in 2007, with a tasting room carved out of the basalt rock on the lower floor, and a 250-person event room and kitchen, which provide space for special events above. The Bryans' passion continues to grow with a 15-acre outdoor special event space and a larger winery production facility added in 2015, and the Cave B Summer Music Theater built in 2017. Although the many seasonal events, including the Grape Stomping Harvest Festival, the Caveman Roar & Pour 5K Trail Fun Run, "B" Inspired Summer Music Theater Series with a special concert series featuring the Yakima Symphony Orchestra, and the Wine Release Dinner, draw guests from around the world, it is the award-winning wines that ultimately garner Cave B the respect and admiration of consumers and critics alike.

Winemaker Freddy Arredondo believes in minimal intervention, and each wine captures the essence of the fruit that's unique to the terroir. With 17 different grape varieties, Cave B produces 25 different wines including; Cabernet Sauvignon, Merlot, Malbec, Syrah, the Bordeaux blend Cuveé du Soleil, wine club exclusive Order of the Cave, Chardonnay, Sauvignon Blanc, Riesling, Gewurztraminer, Blanc de Blanc sparkling white, and more. Quite simply, there's something for every wine lover at Cave B, and the Bryans and their team look forward to introducing guests to an exceptional wine experience.

TOP: We grow 100+ acres of 17 different varieties of grapes. The oldest was planted in 1980. Pictured here Cabernet Sauvignon, planted in 1985.
Photograph by Carrie Arredondo

BELOW: Our natural basalt walls of our Quincy Tasting Room Cave creates an inviting environment for tastings and special events.
Photograph by Steve Lentz

COLUMBIA CREST WINERY PATERSON

Few wineries represent the iconic, pioneering spirit of the Washington wine industry quite like Columbia Crest Winery. Founded in 1983, Columbia Crest has grown from a small winery, in an unknown area, to one of the most significant wineries in the US and a major force behind Washington State's emergence as a world class wine region. It is among the nation's most highly acclaimed wineries and is the only Washington winery to have the honor of receiving *Wine Spectator's* No. 1 Wine in the World ranking on its Top 100 list.

Under the direction of winemaker Juan Muñoz-Oca, Columbia Crest crafts wines that are the product of traditional techniques and innovative technology, as well as Juan's knowledge making wine in world-class regions of Bordeaux, South Australia, Mendoza, and Spain. Juan believes that each wine is about the experience—the nuances of the vineyard and vintage and the expression of the region on the palate. From the thousands of barrels of Grand Estates wines that are hand-stirred weekly to the Reserve wines that are made in the Petit Chai—a separate "winery within the winery"—Columbia Crest produces quality wines that are honest and approachable, even for the burgeoning wine aficionado.

Columbia Crest has the largest vineyard in the state that stretches across 2,500 acres and three tiers of wine—many of which can be sampled at the winery's tasting room throughout the year. Columbia Crest wines capture the best that each varietal has to offer and the essence of the terroir.

LEFT This bold style Cabernet Sauvignon displays great complexity and structure.

ABOVE RIGHT Overlooking the Columbia River, in the heart of the Horse Heaven Hills, Columbia Crest opened its doors in 1983, offering a great atmosphere and selection of highly-acclaimed wines.
Photographs courtesy of Columbia Crest Winery

Den Hoed Wine Estates SEATTLE

Tenacity, family values, and gumption: These principles help define the Washington wine industry, but also describe the journey of the Den Hoed family. Andreas Den Hoed immigrated from Holland to the United States in 1948 with his family. Throughout his teenage years, Andreas was no stranger to hard work, having labored far from home at a dairy farm at age 15 and then later helping his family start a small farm in New Jersey. Although the family had been successful vegetable farmers in Holland, the Dutch government prevented asset removal from the Netherlands, so the Den Hoeds had to build their American business from scratch. By 1953, the family had nearly 500 acres to their name. That year also proved to be fateful for Andreas. Not only did the family take a trip to—and fall in love with—Sunnyside, Washington, but Andreas was also reunited with the love of his life, Marie Christina Kranendonk. Andreas stayed in the Netherlands for six weeks and during that time proposed to Marie on her 20th birthday. When he returned to the US, Andreas and his father set their sights on Washington and purchased a 360-acre farm north of Grandview in the Yakima Valley while he waited for Marie to join him. In 1956, the Den Hoed family planted their first vineyard.

Andreas and Marie were married in 1956, and shortly thereafter, Andreas was drafted into the Army, where he served for two years. His service put his plans for more vineyards on hold for a time, but as soon as Andreas and Marie had the resources to plant more grapes, they never stopped. Each year, the Den Hoeds added to their acreage and in 1988, Andreas' sons, Andy and Bill—who was named Grower of the Year in 2000—were made partners in a new project. As partners, Andreas and his sons added to their acreage in the

FACING PAGE: The diverse topography of Wallula Vineyard was created by the huge Missoula floods that raced down the Columbia River during the last ice age.
Photograph by Andrea Johnson

TOP: A Den Hoed toast as the sun sets at the annual Koning Club event at Wallula Vineyard. Proost!
Photograph by Ron Stephens

CHRISTINA CHARDONNAY

GOURMET PAIRINGS
Pairs well with seared sea scallops with brown butter, caper and lemon sauce.

TASTING NOTES
A graceful balance of stone fruit, acidity, and minerality with a beautiful mid-palate and bright lingering fruit.

WINEMAKER'S INSIGHT
Made from grapes from our estate Kenny Hill Vineyard in the Mill Creek area of the Walla Walla Valley, Christina's complexity, concentration, and purity of fruit embody the best of what the terroir has to offer. Christina is composed of five Dijon clones sourced from Burgundy and planted specifically for this wine. Grapes were gently pressed and co-fermented together before sur lie aging in once-used French oak barrels. A tribute to the personality of Marie Christina Den Hoed, this Chardonnay embodies a well-defined character, balance, and grace.

AWARDS & DISTINCTIONS
92 points – Jeb Dunnuck

TECHNICAL DATA

APPELLATION: Walla Walla Valley
COMPOSITION: 100% Chardonnay
MATURATION: Aged 7 months in once-used French oak
CELLARING: Ready upon release, but can lay down for 5 years or longer

LEARN MORE

Learn more about our wines and winery by scanning the image on the left or visiting www.denhoedwines.com

Yakima Valley, but wanted to expand beyond the area. Finally, in 1997, they purchased 550 acres bordering the Columbia River in the Wallula Gap. The Wallula Vineyard is considered one of the best vineyards in the state, located on south-facing slopes above the Columbia River. The lower elevations of the vineyard are perfect for ultra-premium reds, while acreage above is prime for white varieties.

Today, the Den Hoed vineyards produce a wide range of varietals on over 900 acres, the majority of which are sold to other wineries. Under the careful direction of Washington pioneer winemaker Allen Shoup, the winery produces two Cabernet Sauvignons, a Chardonnay, a sparkling wine, and a Rosé, with future plans to produce additional red wines from Bordeaux and Rhone varieties. The limited production Andreas is a robust Cabernet Sauvignon, crafted by Gilles Nicault. It's a simple, straightforward wine that packs a punch with its vibrant character and awesome backbone. Built with long-term cellaring in mind, Andreas will reach its 20th birthday in fine form.

Den Hoed's other Cabernet Sauvignon, Marie's View, is made from hand-picked grapes, a simple crush, a three-day cold soak, fermentation with hand-punches three times a day, and a hand-press on a wooden basket press. The juice then enters a gravity-fed cellar and ages three years in a mix of new and

TOP: A display of bottles and boxes on the overlook deck at Wallula Vineyard. *Photograph by Ron Stephens*

RIGHT: Terraced Merlot vines in Block 24 thriving alongside the Columbia River. *Photograph by Richard Duval*

used French oak before ultimately assimilating in a 500-gallon French oak tank. The winemaking team likens its style to a small backstage jam session with B.B. King, Ray Charles, Lady Gaga, and Stevie Ray Vaughn. Winemaker Rob Newsom is known for his rich Cabernet Sauvignons, and Marie's View is no different.

On the lighter side, the Christina Chardonnay is a tribute to the personality of Marie Christina Den Hoed: graceful and balanced. Proost, a sparkling wine, whose name comes from the common form of "cheers" in Dutch, is a zero-dosage Blanc de Blancs produced from Chardonnay grapes in the Méthode Champenoise style. The Rosé is light and refreshing, and is made with estate Cinsaut grapes; a variety known for possessing high fruit character and low tannins.

Each year, the winery participates in a variety of local events and treats wine club members to the annual Koning Club event at Wallula Vineyard in September. The Spring Release at the Prosser River Ranch in the heart of Washington wine country is a must for wine club members, and the SoDo tasting room is open to the public. If you want a peek at behind-the-scenes processes at the vineyard, private tours are offered exclusively to Koning Club Members.

TOP: An expansive view of the incomparable Wallula Vineyard in the Horse Heaven Hills with elevations from 320 feet to 1367 feet above sea level.
Photograph by Andrea Johnson

BELOW LEFT: Wine club members celebrating good wine, exquisite vineyards and great friends.
Photograph by Ron Stephens

BELOW RIGHT: Rust on the Rails jamming at the annual Koning Club event at Wallula Vineyard.
Photograph by Ron Stephens

ANDREAS CABERNET SAUVIGNON

GOURMET PAIRINGS

Delicious with bacon-wrapped elk tenderloins.

TASTING NOTES

Vibrant, dark and juicy with layers of bakers chocolate, graphite, leather and dust leading the finish into a long and vibrant journey that calls for one more swallow, and one more…until the bottle is gone.

WINEMAKER'S INSIGHT

The Wallula Vineyard is considered by some to be the best vineyard in the state. Our Andreas Cabernet Sauvignon grapes hail from this vineyard, nestled high above the mighty Columbia River. With such exquisite grapes, very little is needed to create a great wine. Instead, I like to nurture it along in order make a wine that will best showcase a sense of place.

AWARDS & DISTINCTIONS

"It could pass for a cult Cab from one of Napa's great boutiques." – Wine Enthusiast
#4 Seattle Met Top 100 wines of 2014
95+ points–Wine Advocate
2016 Seattle Magazine Winemaker of the Year: Gilles Nicault

TECHNICAL DATA

APPELLATION: Horse Heaven Hills
COMPOSITION: 100% Cabernet Sauvignon
MATURATION: Aged 30 months in 90% new Vicard oak barrels
CELLARING: Excellent upon release but will easily lay down for 15 years and possibly more, depending on the vintage.

ORDER OUR WINE

Visit our wine store by scanning the image to left

FIELDING HILLS WINERY LAKE CHELAN

For the proprietors of Fielding Hills Winery, wine is a personal matter. As a family-owned, multi-generational operation, Fielding Hills Winery's story begins with Isham "Ike" Fielding Wade in 1919 as he set off from Tennessee and settled in the Wenatchee Valley of Washington State. Here he planted the family's first orchards and began the Wade family's agricultural heritage. In 1948, Ike launched an apple and cherry packing business, Columbia Fruit Packers, and began shipping fresh fruit nationally from tiny Wenatchee, Washington. In 1950 Ike's son, Jim joined the company and in 1979 his grandson Mike Wade followed his grandfather and father into the business.

Today, Mike is the CEO of Columbia Fruit Packers and is the founder, owner, and winemaker at Fielding Hills with his wife and general manager Karen. Their three daughters have grown up in this rural agricultural family and have been involved with the winemaking throughout their lives. Today, they are still drawn to Fielding Hills Winery and make time in their professional careers to be involved.

Fielding Hills Winery is an estate winery; the Wade family owns and grows the grapes and does all aspects of winemaking from crush to bottling. In the mid-1990s some of Washington's biggest wineries asked Mike to plant wine grapes. At that time Red Delicious apples were losing their market share, so Mike pulled out 23 acres and created Riverbend Vineyard. Initially Riverbend grew Cabernet Sauvignon and Merlot; Syrah, Cabernet Franc, Malbec, and Carmenere were added later.

FACING PAGE: Fielding Hills Winery glows in the morning sun surrounded by Syrah grapes. The Cascade Mountains to the North overlook expansive views of Lake Chelan from the tasting room.

ABOVE: The tasting room grounds at Fielding Hills Winery provide a spectacular setting for enjoying amazing wines and taking memorable photographs. Mike and Karen Wade take a moment to enjoy the view with wine dogs Ace and Murphie. *Photographs by Patrick Bennett*

The winery produced its first commercial vintage in 2000, using their Wahluke Slope AVA fruit from Estate Riverbend Vineyard. Mike combined his love of agriculture with his passion for wine and gave the winery a name that would honor the family lineage. Fielding Hills Winery produced 400 cases of Cabernet Sauvignon, Merlot, and a red table wine in 2000. He was named Washington State's Rising Star winemaker by Wine Spectator with that first vintage. Mike and Karen, together with family and friends, produced Fielding Hills in an orchard warehouse at their family home. Mike increased production after the initial vintage but interest continued to grow and the demand for Fielding Hills surpassed production ability at the orchard warehouse. In 2014, the operation expanded and they built a tasting room and production facility along the shores of Lake Chelan in Washington State.

Today, Mike and Karen produce about 2,800 cases of world class wines annually. Mike's vision for Fielding Hills has always been to make wines that he and his family would enjoy. This has produced bold, well-balanced reds with a focus on the fruit and the high quality of grapes. The wines are typically aged 22 months in 70 percent new French and American oak with the winemaker recommendation of enjoying the wines in four to seven years from the vintage date. As production increased, an assistant winemaker joined the team: Tyler Armour. He brought knowledge of making Rosé and white wines that complemented Mike's strong red know-how.

TOP: Harvest from the crush pad at Fielding Hills Winery. Visitors in the Fall can gain firsthand knowledge of all the "crush" activities.

BELOW: Crush days can be long and go from sunrise to sunset. Owner Winemaker Mike Wade inspects grapes as they enter the stemmer crusher as the sun sets.
Photographs by Patrick Bennett

RIVERBEND VINEYARD
CABERNET SAUVIGNON

GOURMET PAIRINGS

Pairs well with grilled meats such as filet mignon and ribeye steaks.

TASTING NOTES

With a vibrant, deep ruby color, this wine is bursting with aromas of ripe blackberry, raspberry, and plum. Fresh fruit aromas are balanced by dark cocoa, vanilla, and baking spices. It's a medium-bodied, fruit-forward wine that has fine, powdery tannins and integrated oak.

WINEMAKER'S INSIGHT

All grapes are hand harvested from our Estate Riverbend Vineyard located in the heart of the Wahluke Slope AVA. Once at the winery, the clusters are hand sorted before being destemmed and gently crushed into small one-ton fermenters. The must is cold-soaked overnight and inoculated the following day with selected yeast strains. Twice a day, the must is checked and punched-down to ensure proper extraction. When nearly dry, the free-run wine is transferred directly into oak barrels.

AWARDS & DISTINCTIONS

Wine Enthusiast Magazine, Top 100 Best Wines of the World
Seattle Met Magazine, #1 Washington State Cabernet Sauvignon

TECHNICAL DATA

APPELLATION: Wahluke Slope
COMPOSITION: 86% Cabernet Sauvignon, 8% Syrah, 4% Merlot, 2% Cabernet Franc
MATURATION: The wine is aged for 22 months in a mixture of French and American oak barrels and French puncheons, 70% new oak
CELLARING: Drinks well now, but can be cellared optimally for the next four to seven years

LEARN MORE

Visit our website by scanning the image on the left

The team's obvious talent for creating red wines led to the vision of producing a white wine program. In 2016 Riverview Vineyard was planted. Riverview is the southernmost vineyard in the Wahluke Slope AVA and is home to Chardonnay, Roussanne, and Chenin Blanc.

The traditional Northwest winery and tasting room offers some of the region's best views, plus a tasting menu with wines by the glass. Guests also have the option to enjoy small bites of cheese, crackers, chocolates, and charcuterie. Fielding Hills participates in festivals and holds events throughout the year, including Winterfest in January, Red Wine and Chocolate in February, and Spring Release in April.

At Fielding Hills Winery, the family believes that a glass of wine takes you on a journey. With one sip, the unique story of its land and its people unfold.

FACING PAGE TOP: Guests are welcomed along the path to Fielding Hills' tasting room in summer by lavender and grape vines.
Photograph by Megan Wade

FACING PAGE BOTTOM: There is room for all at the 360-degree circular tasting bar at Fielding Hills. Guests enjoy world class wines paired with a 270-degree view of Lake Chelan.
Photograph by Patrick Bennett

TOP: The outdoor area at Fielding Hills' tasting room has cozy nook seating to enjoy wonderful wines and friends. Guests love lounging on the lawn surrounded by vineyards.
Photograph by Patrick Bennett

BELOW: Murphie, one of the wine dogs at Fielding Hills demonstrates pure enjoyment of life.
Photograph by Patrick Bennett

HAMILTON CELLARS BENTON CITY

When Stacie and Russ Hamilton began considering retirement, they realized that, instead of golfing or fishing, their true passions laid in traveling and wine tasting. Perhaps unsurprisingly, Stacie, a CPA, looked for ways to make both travel and wine tasting tax deductible. The logical answer was, of course, owning a winery, but it was just an idea for a time. It wasn't until the pair watched the sunset over acres of vineyards from a balcony while on a wine tour in 2005, that they realized their dream. It was such a beautiful moment of serenity and connection for the pair that they looked at each other and at the same time said, "Let's do this!" As long-time lovers of wine, Stacie and Russ sought a winemaker whose style and palate reflected their own. Charlie Hoppes had been the expert behind the Hamiltons' favorite wines for many years, so when Hamilton Cellars became a reality, the pair was thrilled to add Charlie to the team as winemaker.

A graduate of UC Davis, Charlie Hoppes spent more than 20 years as a leading winemaker for several notable Washington wineries, including Chateau Ste. Michelle, where he helped craft the first two vintages of Col Solare, the winery's premium label, as head red winemaker. In 1999, Charlie helped found Three Rivers Winery in Walla Walla, and established his own label, Fidelitas Wines in 2000. Charlie consults wineries across the region, and the Hamiltons are proud to count him among their valued partners in crafting truly exceptional wine.

FACING PAGE: The 10-acre vineyard and a portion of the landscaping is viewed from the owner's deck at Hamilton Cellars Estate.

ABOVE The front entrance to the tasting room and the outdoor patio greets our guests at Hamilton Cellars.
Photograph by Stacie Hamilton

TOP: Another beautiful sunset at Hamilton Cellars frames Rattlesnake Mountain, the highest treeless mountain in the United States.

BELOW: Millie, a restored 1946 Chevy truck, our mascot, receives a great deal of attention at the front of the Hamilton Cellars winery.
Photograph by Stacie Hamilton

After struggling to find a home for their winery over several years—the pair were involved in Hollywood-worthy challenges to land rights for a time—Stacie and Russ opened Hamilton Cellars' first tasting room in 2011. Then in September 2014, the Hamiltons were finally able to realize their dream of owning a vineyard on Red Mountain. Today, they live and work on Red Mountain, where their Frank Lloyd Wright-inspired tasting room welcomes guests eager to learn about Washington wine. With over 10 acres of Malbec, Cabernet Sauvignon, Petit Verdot, Cabernet Franc, and Merlot varietals planted at the Hamiltons' winery Bel Tramanto, which translates to "beautiful sunset," the vineyard consistently produces captivating, award-winning wines that reflect the spirit of the region. Guests love the annual events at the winery, including Porks & Corks blending contest for wine club members in April, and Cheeseburgers in Paradise in August. Premier landscaping and the spectacular view of Red Mountain make the winery and tasting room perfect for weddings and outdoor celebrations.

RED MOUNTAIN MALBEC

GOURMET PAIRINGS
This big wine pairs perfectly with high-quality ribeye steak topped with blue cheese.

TASTING NOTES
Red Mountain has produced many celebrated wines, and this Malbec has joined their ranks. Full-bodied with flavors of black cherry, pepper, and chocolate, the wine features great structure with soft tannins and balanced acidity. Oak contributes subtle vanilla notes and a great mouthfeel.

WINEMAKER'S INSIGHT
Malbec is especially well-suited for the soils of Red Mountain, benefitting from the unique minerality contained in Warren loam. The diurnal shift—high daytime temperatures and cool evening temperatures—and long growing season allows the fruit to fully ripen and gain perfect balance. This wine is fermented in large format oak roller barrels, which contributes to soft tannins and a complex finish.

AWARDS AND DISTINCTIONS
Named one of the top four Malbecs in Washington State – Tasting Room Magazine;
Double gold medal – Seattle Wine Awards

TECHNICAL DATA

APPELLATION: Red Mountain
COMPOSITION: 100% Malbec
MATURATION: Aged 22 months in a combination of new American oak barrels and neutral French oak barrels.
CELLARING: : Delicious now and exceptional if cellared for up to 15 years

VISIT OUR STORE

Enter our store by scanning image on left or visit www.securewineshop.net/hamiltoncellars

HEDGES FAMILY ESTATE BENTON CITY

Soil meets soul at Hedges Family Estate, where the blend of rich cultural upbringings and a shared love for creating beautiful wine converge at the heart of the bucolic Red Mountain. Led by a passion for authenticity and a deep connection to the land they call home, the Hedges family epitomizes the modern wine estate by uniting past and present, as they continue to evolve the winemaking tradition for generations to come.

Tending to the riches of Red Mountain with a visionary blend of biodynamic farming and time-honored winemaking techniques, Hedges Family Estate lends an ear to the earth and a voice to the vines. Their wines are testament to their dedication to letting the land speak for itself. It's something that has been important to owners Tom and Anne-Marie Hedges from the beginning—even when they started their wine adventure in 1987 with American Wine Trade, Inc., exporting Washington and California wine worldwide. They realized the Washington wine industry was about to boom and they wanted to be a part of it by growing and making their own wine.

Anne-Marie grew up in France, where she witnessed from an early age the beauty of small-estate winemakers through her grandfather, who was passionate about fine wine. Perhaps it was fate when Tom ran into vineyard owner Fred Artz at his 20th high school reunion in 1989. Fred introduced the Hedges to a 50-acre parcel of land on Red Mountain the day after that reunion—and the seeds of the vineyard were born. About six years later, the Hedges broke ground on the winery—designed in the manner of a French-inspired Bordeaux chateau—continuing the evolution of the family business.

FACING PAGE: The grand entrance to the Hedges Family Estate chateau on Red Mountain.

TOP: Gazing up towards the Chateau from the Demeter-certified Biodynamic Cabernet Sauvignon vines–Hedges vineyard
Photographs by Richard Duval

They grew the estate to 120 acres in the Red Mountain AVA and continue to be stewards of this great land by producing wines with a global audience.

Now, the beautifully landscaped winery not only features a comfortable tasting area, but also a French farm kitchen and an enclosed stone veranda referred to as the Champagne salon— all replete with rustic charm. To complete the Old-World aura, the biodynamic farm also includes a chicken chateau with a courtyard adjacent to the organic garden and tranquil pond.

No wonder Hedges Family Estate has been voted as one of only five American wineries that make you think you are in Europe (the other four being in Napa Valley).

TOP LEFT: Three generations of Hedges dedicated to preserving and promoting the terroir of Red Mountain.

TOP RIGHT: Tom and Anne-Marie Hedges have created a life around building a legacy on Red Mountain.

BELOW LEFT: The second generation is taking cues from history to bring Hedges Family Estate into the future.

BELOW RIGHT: The beautifully manicured front lawn of the estate.
Photographs by Richard Duval

BIODYNAMIC SYRAH

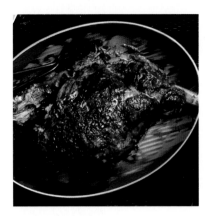

GOURMET PAIRINGS

Slow-roasted leg of lamb, infused with garlic and rosemary, is a perfect match for this Syrah.

TASTING NOTES

Deeply hued with a dark, inky purple color, the Hedges Family Estate Biodynamic Syrah features hints of wild game, cinnamon, cloves, dried blueberry, and a slight hint of vanilla. Very rich on the palate, this wine fills the mouth with an intense rush of flavor. Its lush finish provides satisfaction with every sip. This is a great example of the power and elegance of Red Mountain Syrah.

WINEMAKER'S INSIGHT

Grapes from the Hedges Estate Biodynamic vineyard are hand-harvested and crushed into bins, where they undergo native yeast fermentation. The must is punched down by hand three times a day until the desired mouthfeel and flavors are achieved. After pressing the wine, it is aged in barrel and undergoes native malolactic fermentation.

TECHNICAL DATA

APPELLATION: Red Mountain
COMPOSITION: 100% Biodynamic Syrah
MATURATION: Ten months in 67% new oak, 50% French, and 50% American barrels
CELLARING: Lovely upon release, developing as long as 10-plus years

LEARN MORE

Learn more about this wine and our winery by scanning the image on the left

CABERNET SAUVIGNON, RED MOUNTAIN

GOURMET PAIRINGS

Coq-au-vin—chicken slowly simmered in a rich red wine and mushroom sauce—is a Hedges winery favorite. This French version of comfort food is ideal with this Cabernet Sauvignon.

TASTING NOTES

Boasting a brilliant red garnet color, the Hedges Family Estate Cabernet Sauvignon explodes with bright blackberry and cassis notes along with leather, fresh earth, cocoa powder, cinnamon, vanilla bean, and dried herbs, balancing perfectly with the noticeable yet disciplined tannins. It's a tantalizing blend of intense fruit, spice, and savory herbs that is lively with a serious mid-palate and finish.

WINEMAKER'S INSIGHT

The fruit is sourced from Hedges, Jolet, Bel' Villa, and Magdalena vineyards on Red Mountain. This wine is cold-soaked overnight then inoculated with yeast and fermented for seven to 10 days on skins while being pumped over twice daily before pressing to barrels, where it undergoes malolactic fermentation and aging.

AWARDS AND DISTINCTIONS

92 points – Wine Advocate

TECHNICAL DATA

APPELLATION: Red Mountain
COMPOSITION: 75-100% Cabernet Sauvignon—varying with vintage
MATURATION: Nineteen months in 41% new oak, 18% French, and 82% American barrels
CELLARING: Drinkable upon release, but developing as long as 15-20 years

VISIT OUR STORE

Buy this wine by scanning image on left

TOP LEFT & RIGHT: Looking south from the Champagne Salon. A perfect place to savor a great bottle of Champagne

BELOW: The high-density plantings of Hedges Demeter-certified old vineyard.
Photographs by Richard Duval

RED MOUNTAIN BLEND

GOURMET PAIRINGS

A rustic, savory ratatouille tart filled with stewed Provençal-style summer vegetables. The earthy eggplant and vibrant tomato against a flaky tart are the perfect backdrop for this wine to shine.

TASTING NOTES

The dark, purple-black color alludes to this blend's aromas of black cherry, blackberry, anise, nutmeg, dried ginger, and cinnamon. Hints of pomegranate and dark cocoa also play on the palate with just a touch of aged leather. In the mouth, this wine is full with nicely balanced acidity. Flavors of earthy fruit and toasted hazelnut linger into a lush and satisfying finish. It's a cozy-up-to-the-fire kind of wine.

WINEMAKER'S INSIGHT

This blend's grapes hail from Hedges, Jolet, Bel' Villa, Les Gosses, and Magdalena vineyards on Red Mountain. The grapes are destemmed and partially crushed into stainless steel fermenters. The must is pumped over twice daily until desired tannin extraction is achieved and then gently pressed to barrels where it undergoes malolactic fermentation and aging.

AWARDS AND DISTINCTIONS

90 points – Wine Advocate

TECHNICAL DATA

APPELLATION: Red Mountain

COMPOSITION: Typically, a majority of Cabernet Sauvignon, followed by Merlot and rounded out with Syrah, Cabernet Franc, Malbec, and Petit Verdot

MATURATION: Twenty months in 40% new oak, 35% French oak, and 65% American barrels

CELLARING: Drinkable upon release; enjoyable up to 10-plus years

VISIT OUR STORE

Buy this wine by scanning image on left

LA HAUTE CUVÉE BIODYNAMIC CABERNET SAUVIGNON

GOURMET PAIRINGS

The ultimate cheese plate with Camembert, Reblochon, Tomme de Savoie, and Taleggio is a beloved tradition at the Chateau to end each meal—until the last drop of wine is gone!

TASTING NOTES

The gorgeous, garnet color hints at the super-intense flavors of fig, cassis, and rosemary. The bright and full entry dances on the palate, as it sends shots of blackberry, black pepper, cinnamon, and earthy cocoa flavors, ending with an intensely structured, full finish. A wildly complex, savage Cabernet Sauvignon, it will mellow on the palate over the next 10 to 20 years and seems to constantly change with every sniff and taste.

WINEMAKER'S INSIGHT

The grapes are from the biodynamic Hedges Old Vine Vineyard and Magdalena Vineyard. The grapes were destemmed and partially crushed into stainless steel fermenters, where it was allowed to begin fermenting with native yeast. It was pumped over twice daily until desired tannin extraction was achieved. It was then pressed to barrels where it underwent native malolactic fermentation and aging.

AWARDS & DISTINCTIONS

93 points – Wine Advocate
93 points – Wine Spectator

TECHNICAL DATA

APPELLATION: Red Mountain
COMPOSITION: 100% Biodynamic Cabernet Sauvignon
MATURATION: Eighteen months in 20% new oak, 100% American oak barrels
CELLARING: Drinks well within five to 10 years of the vintage date, but can age up to 20 years

LEARN MORE

Learn more about this wine and our winery by scanning the image on the left

J. BOOKWALTER WINERY RICHLAND

A close relationship with the land runs deep in the Bookwalter family—10 generations of the family have been involved in American agriculture. But when it was Jerry Bookwalter's turn to cultivate the land, he brought the family into its next phase: viticulture. After graduating from UC Davis in 1963, Jerry spent 13 years farming in California's San Joaquin Valley before moving his family to Washington in 1976. Once there, Jerry began making a name for Bookwalter in the burgeoning wine industry and managed the three iconic vineyards Sagemoor, Bacchus, and Dionysus. Jerry would go on to be vineyard manager at famed Conner Lee Vineyard and in 1983 began J. Bookwalter Winery.

Today, Jerry's son John serves as president of the winery. He literally grew up in the vineyards, and in 1997 joined the family winery and soon took over winemaking responsibilities. World-renowned consulting winemakers Zelma Long and Claude Gros were hired in 2000 and 2008 respectively, and the winery received an image refresh to take it into the next century. Acclaimed winemaker Caleb Foster took over most of the winemaking responsibilities in 2014, but it's not uncommon to see John in the cellar or visiting the tasting room.

With the knowledge that great wine comes from exceptional grapes, J. Bookwalter crafts wines from some of the oldest established vineyards in Washington. Over half of the winery's grapes come from the Conner Lee Vineyard, where the Bookwalters have enjoyed a relationship for nearly three decades.

FACING PAGE: The talent behind our wines; Caleb Foster Winemaker, John Bookwalter Owner.

TOP LEFT: The distinctive J. Bookwalter branding on French oak barrels for red wine aging.

TOP RIGHT: Vineyard block placard in the Conner-Lee Vineyard in Othello, Washington.
Photographs by Kim Fetrow

DOUBLE PLOT CHARDONNAY

GOURMET PAIRINGS

Perfect with pan-roasted Pacific Cod topped with smoked Columbia River Steelhead mousse and herb-parmesan breadcrumb crust, served with parsnip puree, sherried Brussels Sprouts, and pine nuts.

TASTING NOTES

Aromas of Meyer lemon, flower, Anjou pears, and crème brûlée mingle in the Double Plot Chardonnay. A restrained, young wine, it opens to show abundant sweet fruit and rich persistent lemony flavors. The Chardonnay is pale yellow in color and offers ripe flavors and fresh acidity—perfect for savory fish and vegetable dishes.

WINEMAKER'S INSIGHT

Fruit from the Conner Lee Vineyard improves year over year. We selected fruit from the 1989 old block and the newer clone #75 for this Chardonnay. The fruit was whole-cluster pressed before being fermented and aged in Burgundy puncheons on its lees for 10 months. Just before bottling, the wine was blended and filtered. Bottled for freshness, this wine is best served above fridge temperature at 50°F.

AWARDS & DISTINCTIONS

93 points – Tastings

TECHNICAL DATA

APPELLATION: Columbia Valley
COMPOSITION: 100% Chardonnay
MATURATION: Aged 10 months in 100% Burgundy puncheons
CELLARING: Enjoy upon release and for five years or more

ORDER OUR WINE

Visit our wine store by scanning the image to left

The oldest blocks of Cabernet Sauvignon from 1987, 1988, and 1991, as well as the 1992 block of Merlot, provide grapes for J. Bookwalter wines. Other varietals harvested from this vineyard include Cabernet Franc, Syrah, Malbec, and Chardonnay. The Elephant Mountain Vineyard provides the winery with incredible Cabernets and Syrahs from its unique microclimate, while the Bacchus and Dionysus Vineyards from the Sagemoor group provide even more outstanding Cabernet Sauvignon, Merlot, and a Neustadt clone Riesling. Each wine sports a literary name—Suspense, Protagonist, Conflict, Antagonist—and each boasts its own set of acclaim and awards.

Named among the best wineries to visit by Food & Wine magazine, a top-nine winery with fabulous food by Zagat Guide, and with 94 points for the Chapter 7 Cabernet

TOP: The view of our grounds and the vineyard from the side patio at J. Bookwalter Winery in Richland
Photograph by Kim Fetrow

RIGHT: Gretchen and John Bookwalter during the Auction of Washington Wine at Chateau Ste. Michelle in Woodinville.
Photograph by Richard Duval

Sauvignon, it's clear that the Bookwalters know their wine. A visit to the winery and Fiction @ J. Bookwalter, the winery's restaurant, enhances the wine experience—staff members are ready to recommend a J. Bookwalter wine for whatever dish tickles your taste buds.

Lunch includes delectable options including the Duck Confit Salad, a Smoked Gouda Burger, and the mouth-watering Pig & Pickle—slow roasted pork, bacon, aioli, arugula, pickled shishito peppers, blue cheese, and apple preserves on a toasted baguette. At dinner, indulge in the PNW Wild Mushroom & Herb Risotto, Snake River Wagyu Short Ribs, or Smoked Chicken Mac 'N' Cheese. Brunch is held every Sunday. At the craft bar, Fable, the bartenders serve signature and classic cocktails in the sophisticated, yet rustic, atmosphere.

In the mood for a tasting only? Visit Woodinville Tasting Studio where the team is ready to tell you the story of J. Bookwalter wines as you sip and sample.

TOP: The front patio at J. Bookwater Winery is a popular spot for our wine tasting visitors.

ABOVE: Protagonist Cabernet Sauvignon.
Photographs by Kim Fetrow

CHAPTER 7 CABERNET SAUVIGNON

GOURMET PAIRINGS

Perfect with with osso bucco.

TASTING NOTES

Aromas that can only be described as hedonistic invite you into this lush wine. Mocha, spices, graphite, and ripe black fruits build the complex and savory wine to a powerful finish. Our old vine selection of Conner Lee Vineyard's Cabernet Sauvignon expresses its age-worthy perfection in this wine. Dense flavors, smooth tannins, and refreshing acidity are what fruit from this vineyard have become known for.

WINEMAKER'S INSIGHT

Handpicked in the morning hours of early October, the Merlot and Syrah are fermented in puncheons with free run selected for the cuvée. Cabernet Sauvignons from 1987 and 1988 fully ripened under the waxing October full moon. All clusters were hand-sorted, destemmed, and resorted. Each went into its own fermenter, where they were chilled and cold soaked for three days to develop richness and smooth tannins. Hand-mixed daily for two weeks on skins, only free run was selected for aging in puncheons. The wine was stirred and aged on lees to develop savory tones that complement the powerful fruit. After 18 months, we blended each selected puncheon and barrel for this rare wine.

AWARDS AND DISTINCTIONS

94 points – Wine Spectator

TECHNICAL DATA

APPELLATION: Columbia Valley

COMPOSITION: 90% Cabernet Sauvignon, 3% Syrah, 3% Malbec, 2% Merlot, 2% Cabernet Franc

MATURATION: Aged 18 months in 100% new French Bordeaux puncheons

CELLARING: Enjoy upon release and for decades to come

VISIT OUR STORE

Buy this wine by scanning image on left

177

MARKET VINEYARDS RICHLAND

If you could bottle passion and commitment, it would probably have the flavor and body of a Market Vineyards wine. The team is driven by these two qualities, and it shows up in every bottle, offering drinkers standout wines that are hard to come by.

Steve Anderson, Bob Bertsch, Kelly Precechtel Bright, Matt Riesenweber, and Dan Schulte opened Market Vineyards in 2008 with the notion that high standards must be maintained at every step of the winemaking process. Harvested in the Columbia Valley and Red Mountain growing regions, the grapes for Market Vineyards' wines are hand-picked with careful attention to detail. Market Vineyards has established a longstanding relationship with Red Mountain vineyards, allowing the winery to select, blend, and highlight the best regional fruit. Winemaker Charlie Hoppes—one of Washington's best—uses American and custom French oak barrels, all hand-selected, to age the wines for anywhere from 22 to 36 months. Bold merlots, full-bodied cabernets, and memorable Bordeaux-style wines are the results.

There are tasting rooms in both Richland and Woodinville where guests can sample an array of varietals. But if you're looking to really taste the good stuff, you'd be wise to join the Market Vineyards Wine Club. It features exclusive bottles for members only with biannual releases. Syrah, Malbec, Cabernet, and Merlot for instance, are produced from 100 percent Red Mountain grapes and available to members only through special releases. You can opt for either the Bear or Bull Market Club—aptly named after the partners' years of

LEFT Produced with passion, Market Vineyards' wine exemplifies the best Washington State has to offer. *Photograph by Sara Nelson*

ABOVE: Located at the heart of the Red Mountain AVA, Ciel du Cheval Vineyards is one of the acclaimed vineyards where Market Vineyards sources fruit. *Photograph by Jason Tomlinson*

working in the financial industry. The Bear Market Club offers 12 bottles per year, while the Bull has 24. Both have big wine savings, and include complimentary tastings, access to limited production and library wines, plus advance invitations to all of the club events. Members will get to sample the Unicorn release, an edition which will sell out quickly and is named after the stock market term for companies worth a billion dollars or more. Other market references include wine names such as Acquisition, Dividend, Merval—Argentina's stock exchange, Derivative, and Basis Points. Over the years, the clubs have gained a loyal following, with some members belonging since the winery's inception.

With the intent of always keeping a boutique feel, Market Vineyards produces roughly 3,000 cases annually. The idea is to keep an eye on a smaller production to maintain the highest quality and attention to detail. This approach has gotten some attention, as Market Vineyards wines have been served at James Beard dinner events by some of the country's top restaurants.

Market Vineyards also features ideal space for events, including weddings, reunions, meetings, and parties. The venue is intimate, scenic, and obviously has some of the Washington's best wines on hand.

TOP: The interior of the Market Vineyards tasting room in Woodinville, located behind the historic Hollywood Schoolhouse.
Photograph by Jason Tomlinson

MIDDLE: Acquisition Cabernet Sauvignon, one of several Red Mountain wines produced exclusively for wine club members.
Photograph by Sara Nelson

BOTTOM: The outdoor seating area in front of the Market Vineyards Woodinville tasting room.
Photograph by Richard Duval

ALPHA MERLOT

GOURMET PAIRINGS

Pairs well with a wide range of foods, from desserts to Kansas City grass-fed beef. Complements Washington-caught seafood especially well, and stands up to spicy paella.

TASTING NOTES

Illustrating exceptional depth and color, the aromas are rich and plentiful revealing dark fruit tones with a hint of caramel, vanilla bean and assorted barrel spices. The dense palate is layered with plentiful rich flavors of dark cherry and rich plum. The wine illustrates excellent complexity and solid structure while offering supple and refined tannins which lead to an elegant finish.

WINEMAKER'S INSIGHT

Known for hot days and cool nights, Red Mountain produces exceptional fruit which is handpicked and sorted and illustrates incredible intensity and concentration. It showcases what Washington State Merlots have become known for, leveraging the tradition of Merlot and exemplifying what Red Mountain has to offer. The attention to detail is not just noticed in the fruit, but also in the artistic abilities in the cellar. Custom French and American barrels are hand-selected and properly matched for each vintage.

AWARDS & DISTINCTIONS

93 points – Wine Enthusiast Magazine
Selected as one of the wines representing Washington State at the Wine Spectator luncheon in New York City.

TECHNICAL DATA

APPELLATION: Red Mountain
COMPOSITION: 100% Merlot
MATURATION: Aged 24 months in 100% French oak barrels, once used
CELLARING: Years from peak expression, the wine will age gracefully and continue to do so for years to come

LEARN MORE

Visit our website by scanning the image on the left

MERCER WINE ESTATES PROSSER

Wine is a family affair at Mercer Wine Estates, founded by brothers Rob and Will Mercer in 2005. Hailing from a family with a rich agricultural history— they began farming the land in 1886—the Mercer family began turning water into wine, as they say, in 1968. It was then that irrigation was introduced to Mercer Ranches, Inc., and formed the foundation for the growth of crops, including wine grapes. In 1972, Rob and Will's uncle and aunt, Don and Linda Mercer, became the founding grape growers in Horse Heaven Hills. They planted Cabernet Sauvignon grapes in Block 1, which would later become the acclaimed Champoux Vineyard.

The first vintage of Mercer Wine Estates was released in 2005 with a small batch each of Cabernet Sauvignon and Merlot. In 2009, the tasting room opened. In more recent years, the winery has expanded to include a premier vineyard site, Chapman Creek. In 2016, Wine Press Northwest named Mercer Washington Winery of the Year. Also in 2016, Mercer garnered acclaim in Texas at the Houston International Wine Competition where the winery received awards for Top Pacific Northwest Wine and Top Red Wine—along with a custom saddle and chaps.

With two tasting rooms where guest can sample the Mercer Wine Estates' portfolio of wines—one in Seattle and another in Prosser—the Mercers love introducing people to their unique offerings. Mercer wines include Sauvignon Blanc, Riesling, Viognier, Chardonnay, Rosé, Merlot, Malbec, Cabernet Sauvignon, Mourvedre, Grenache, Petit Verdot, Syrah, and three red blends: the proprietary blend, a Bordeaux-style blend, and a Rhone-style blend.

FACING PAGE: Founding brothers, Will and Rob Mercer in the barrel room in Horse Heaven Hills.
Photograph by Andrea Johnson

ABOVE: Overlooking the Mercer Ranches and Horse Heaven Hills vineyards.
Photograph by T.J. Mercer

ESTATES CABERNET SAUVIGNON

GOURMET PAIRINGS

Nothing compares to your favorite cut of meat, a loaded baked potato and a healthy vegetable like Mercer Cabernet Sauvignon.

TASTING NOTES

Aromas of blackberry, dark plum, and blackberry jam blend with hints of sweet caramel and cocoa powder. In the palate, the ripe fruit is framed by powdery tannins. The well-integrated oak and dusty tannins lead into a velvety finish with a nice touch of acidity on the end. This wine is a lovely balance of power and grace.

WINEMAKER'S INSIGHT

Our grapes are double sorted, first in the vineyard with the selective harvest on our Pellenc harvesters, then again at the winery on our sorting table. The fruit was not crushed in order to preserve as much whole-berry as possible. At the winery, individual lots were fermented in stainless steel tanks. Twice daily pumpovers allowed gentle extraction of color and tannins. After draining the wine and pressing the skins, the wine was racked to a blend of French and American oak barrels for malolactic fermentation.

AWARDS & DISTINCTIONS

Best Red Wine – Seattle Wine Awards
Double-Gold & Best of Class – Seattle Wine Awards
Best Pacific Northwest Wine (Saddle Winner) – Houston Livestock Show and Rodeo Wine Competition
90 pts – Wine Advocate

TECHNICAL DATA

APPELLATION: Horse Heaven Hills
COMPOSITION: Primarily Cabernet Sauvignon with small percentages of Syrah, Merlot, and Petit Verdot
MATURATION: Aged 20 months in French and American oak.
CELLARING: Enjoy now, to up to 10 years cellar time from vintage date

LEARN MORE

Learn more about our wines and winery by scanning the image on the left or visiting www.mercerwine.com

Each year, Mercer Wine Estates hosts several events open to the public, including the Winter Wine & Dine, Summer BBQ Bash, events in Prosser, and the March Taste Washington Wine Dinner and August Washington Wine Month Dinner and other events in Seattle.

When guests visit the winery facility in Eastern Washington—tours are by appointment—they are delighted by how well the large building gracefully merges with the landscape. Inspired by the desert, the contemporary facility features rich brown tones and ample tinted windows through which guests can view the landscape. The property is also xeriscaped with low-water, drought-tolerant plants including native mock orange and bunch grasses. Sustainability continues at the Seattle tasting room, housed in an old machine and welding shop in the Georgetown neighborhood. The bar was built from old farm equipment, and the décor resonates with the industrial building and surrounding architecture.

Behind the scenes, owners Rob Mercer and Brenda Mercer—who also serves as the Charitable Giving Director and handles public relations—are joined by an exceptional team of experts who share a passion for wine. Will Mercer serves as the Business Development Manager, and Sean Kendall is the General Manager. Winemaker Jeremy Santo and Director of Vineyards, John Derrick, work closely with one another to ensure the wines are consistent with the quality for which Mercer is known.

TOP: Vineyard crew hard at work harvesting Merlot grapes in the Cavalie Vineyard with our Pelleric Harvester.
Photograph by Andrea Johnson

RIGHT: Steel tanks inside with the grape crush pads outside the Mercer Estates production facility in Prosser, Washington.
Photograph by T.J. Mercer

Each of the nine vineyards on Mercer Ranches farm brings its unique characteristics to the Mercer wine portfolio. Spice Cabinet Vineyard sits on 18 acres adjacent to the Columbia River. Its deep sandy soil and steep southeast aspect mimic the characteristics of the Rhone region. The vineyard yields an array of varietals including Grenache, Malbec, Mourvedre, Petit Verdot, Sangiovese, Cabernet Sauvignon, and Syrah.

The five-acre Big Teepee Vineyard sits adjacent to the Mercer family farm. It was initially planted as a landscape improvement site but surprised the family by consistently producing Cabernet Sauvignon of extremely deep color and a healthy dose of rich tannins.

Cavalie Vineyard was named in honor of Captain Alexander Cavalie Mercer, a hero of the Battle of Waterloo. This vineyard is also home to Block 93, dedicated to modern-day heroes of Flight 93, the fourth plane hijacked on September 11, 2001, that went down in rural Pennsylvania.

TOP: At our tasting room, a relaxing environment for enjoying our wine at the bar or at tables on our patio.
Photograph by Andrea Johnson

BELOW LEFT: Artwork used on our labels, by Diane Whitehead, adorn the walls of our Prosser tasting room.
Photograph by Andrea Johnson

BELOW RIGHT: One of two tempature controlled barrel rooms at Mercer Estates Winery.
Photograph by T. J. Mercer

RESERVE CAVALIE

GOURMET PAIRINGS

This hearty Bordeaux style blend pairs beautifully with a meaty pasta Bolognese.

TASTING NOTES

The powerful Merlot is evident in this blend which opens with aromas of ripe blueberries wrapped in the warmth of warm baking spices and sweet caramel. The Cabernet Sauvignon creates a frame of structure while the Malbec adds suppleness, weight, and length. This rich, full-bodied wine is full of intriguing complexity built around sleek tannins that lead to a finish that goes on and on.

WINEMAKER'S INSIGHT

The fruit was machine harvested with our "Selective Harvest" attachment allowing the fruit to be sorted in the vineyard. We bypassed the destemmer to maintain as much whole berry as possible. The grapes were sorted a second time on our sorting table and then fermented in our French Oak tank. After draining the wine and pressing, the wine was racked to a blend of new and old French oak barrels for malolactic fermentation.

AWARDS & DISTINCTIONS

91 points – Wine Advocate
93 points – Tasting Panel
Top Red Wine & Chaps Winner – Houston Livestock & Rodeo Wine Competition

TECHNICAL DATA

APPELLATION: Horse Heaven Hills
COMPOSITION: Primarily Merlot, with Cabernet Sauvignon and Merlot
MATURATION: Aged 22 months in new and old French oak
CELLARING: Enjoy now and for up to 15 years cellar time from vintage date

ORDER OUR WINE

Visit our wine store by scanning the image to left

RESERVE CHARDONNAY

GOURMET PAIRINGS

This Chardonnay is delicious with any meal, but try it with a hearty Arugula salad with salted and candied pecans, cranberries, a vibrant lemony vinagrette and Pecorino cheese.

TASTING NOTES

Aromas of apricot, guava, and pineapple juice mingle with hints of sweet vanilla and warm toasty notes. These flavors continue in the palate and are complemented by a rich, round mouthfeel with a nice balance of acidity due to restrained malolactic fermentation. Barrel fermentation and sur lie aging create a wine that is both elegant and robust. Flavors of caramelized apricots in a honey glaze, dusted with saffron, and served with vanilla bean ice cream continue through the finish.

WINEMAKER'S INSIGHT

The grapes were harvested in the very early hours of the morning so that they would arrive at the winery cool. Once at the winery, the grapes when directly to the press where the juice was gently pressed away from the skins. The juice cold settled for two days before racking and was then fermented in a blend of 50 percent new and 50 percent Burgundian French oak barrels, for approximately one month. We inoculated three of the 10 barrels for malolactic fermentation to help create a creamy mouthfeel while retaining the bright natural acidity of the grapes. The barrels were hand-stirred on a weekly basis over the next four months to help contribute to the creamy, rich mouthfeel.

AWARDS & DISTINCTIONS

Gold – San Francisco Chronical,
Double Gold – Seattle Wine Awards

TECHNICAL DATA

APPELLATION: Horse Heaven Hills, Zephyr Ridge Vineyard
COMPOSITION: 100% Chardonnay
MATURATION: Aged 10 months in 50% new Burgundian French oak barrels
CELLARING: Enjoy now and up to five years from vintage date

ORDER OUR WINE

Visit our store to order this wine and others by scanning the image on the left

Culloden Vineyard was named in honor of the lost Battle of Culloden that provided the impetus for Hugh Mercer to leave Scotland and settle in the New World.

Dead Canyon Vineyard features grapes planted along both edges of the canyon located three miles south of the original Mercer farmstead. The north and south face of the canyon offer two distinct aspects of a similar terroir, featured in Mercer Canyons Cabernet Sauvignon and Red Blend, Estates Cabernet Sauvignon, Estates Sharp Sisters Red Blend, and the Reserve Syrah.

Eagle & Plow is Mercer's largest vineyard site, located at the northwest corner of the family farm. Cabernet Sauvignon grows abundantly here, and the vineyard's name reflects patriotism and hard work, along with optimism for future generations. Finally, Princeton Vineyard pays homage to Brigadier General Hugh Mercer who fought and died at the Battle of Princeton in the American Revolution. The 525-acre, 27-block vineyard is planted with Cabernet Sauvignon and Merlot.

TOP AND RIGHT: Rob Mercer inspecting and admiring the vines at the Big Teepee Vineyard.
Photograph by Andrea Johnson

SAGEMOOR PASCO

When the founding members of Sagemoor made their initial plantings in 1972, they had determination, plenty of grit, and about 400 acres of vines. Today, their land has expanded to encompass more than 1,100 acres with five distinct vineyards: Sagemoor, Bacchus, Dionysus, Gamache, and Weinbau. Collectively, the vineyards now produce 18 varieties including Cabernet Sauvignon, Riesling, Sauvignon Blanc, Syrah, Cabernet Franc, Chardonnay, Malbec, Petit Verdot and Merlot, among others.

Lead by Alec Bayless, Albert Ravenholt, Winslow Wright, and Syd Abrams, the original partnership pioneered, profited, and persevered for more than 40 years to create a renowned vineyard operation. With advice from Walter Clore, the group discovered and planted sites that have stood the test of economics, weather, social change, and time. Since the beginning, vineyard employees collaborated with leadership to make lasting contributions to Sagemoor and the Washington wine industry. Today's management team of Kent Waliser, Lacey Lybeck, Miguel Rodriguez, Miguel Contreras, and Andres Palencia lead detail-oriented employees who know what is necessary to nurture the vineyards and grow premium grapes.

FACING PAGE: Director of Vineyard Operations Kent Waliser oversees harvest of Sauvignon Blanc from Gamache Vineyard as key component of its signature "Without Rehearsal" wine.

TOP: Vineyard Manager Lacey Lybeck regularly walks rows at renowned Bacchus vineyard, tasting grapes to determine harvest timing for each of the 100 wineries using Sagemoor fruit.
Photographs by Richard Duval

In the 1970s, the Washington wine industry was much smaller than it is today and was unable to use much of Sagemoor's fruit. Because so few local wineries existed, the grapes were sold to nearby states and Canadian customers. That's a far cry from the 100-plus wineries that source their grapes from Sagemoor today. These Washington customers seek out Sagemoor to build their brands, many using these vineyard names to enhance their position in the market.

LIMITED RELEASE

WITHOUT REHEARSAL

Sauvignon Blanc / Semillon

COLUMBIA VALLEY

2016

VINEYARDS	DIONYSUS D.20	32%
	BACCHUS B.5	31%
	GAMACHE G.23	37%

WITHOUT REHEARSAL

GOURMET PAIRINGS

This wine pairs masterfully with your favorite fish preparation–we like salmon with a lemon cream sauce.

TASTING NOTES

This wine has a viscous mouthfeel and unreserved minerality. It features a medley of soft melon and palate-tickling citrus zest with a gorgeous balance and a silky smooth finish. We love it alone but even more so with lunch.

WINEMAKER'S INSIGHT

As 2016 harvest approached, we brainstormed our first white wine collaboration. Ali Mayfield helped us achieve our aspirations, and at the end of August in 2016, Lacey Lybeck was standing among rare, unclaimed Sauvignon Blanc in our Bacchus Vineyard. This was the first of three components for Without Rehearsal. Another block of Sauvignon Blanc came up in Gamache Vineyard, then for the crucial Semillon, our Dionysus Vineyard produced rose-gold clusters that tasted like sliced pears. Without Rehearsal is as honest a name as they come.

TECHNICAL DATA

APPELLATION: Columbia Valley
COMPOSITION: 68% Sauvignon Blanc, 32% Semillon
MATURATION: Fermented in stainless steel
CELLARING: Excellent now and will age for up to 5 years after vintage

LEARN MORE

Visit our website by scanning the image to left

TOP LEFT: John Duval, Gilles Nicault, and Kent Waliser admire Syrah from Bacchus grown for Sequel at Long Shadows Vintners.
Photograph by Richaed Duval

RIGHT Ranch Manager Andres Palencia admiring the results of hard work in the vineyard, looking forward to harvest and another great vintage.
Photograph by Richaed Duval

BOTTOM LEFT: Ranch Manger Miguel Rodriguez reflects on selecting which winery his crew will harvest grapes for among the many wineries that source from Weinbau.
Photograph by Kent Waliser

Today's management team increased the number of grape customers and further refined the running of the vineyards to reflect changing market conditions. Sagemoor customers represent the largest of Washington State wineries, as well as boutique operations. Many of the winemaking clients actively participate in viticulture decision-making within their preferred blocks to reach their own flavor-profile goals. Precision farming techniques such as vigor mapping, soil profiling, variety selection, row orientation, and selected harvest techniques are used to manage yields, balance canopy with crop load, optimize sun exposure, and ensure consistent quality fruit.

The variance in soil, climate, and sunlight across the five vineyards gives Sagemoor the ability to coax a range of characteristics from the grapes: from elegant to powerful, with soft or muscular tannins, from dried herbs and spice, to a spectrum of fruit characteristics. As pioneers of Cabernet Sauvignon in

193

Washington State, Sagemoor has Cabernet grapes at every location, with three of them boasting prized 1972 plantings that never experienced a killing freeze. Maintaining these grapes at each of the sites provides a broad range of flavor profiles which helps to fulfill a winemaker's personal vision by offering a dynamic variety. Sauvignon Blanc is another still-vital grape from the 1972 plantings, and has remained incredibly pure at the Bacchus vineyard thanks to beautifully balanced canopies. The oscillation of the hills helps to achieve different styles in a single row. True varietal characteristics appear on the north-facing aspects, and more star fruit on the south-facing. At harvest time, the team picks an exact spot for one winemaker, and the next vine supports a completely different vision of another winemaker.

In 2014, Allan Brothers of Naches, Washington, purchased the vineyards. The family has a long and rich history in the Yakima Valley and has been growing, packing, and shipping premium tree-fruit products since the 1920s. They carry on the Sagemoor legacy as a tribute to the hard work of the original owners and all the employees who made the vineyards what they are today. The vision going forward will enhance the legacy of Sagemoor as an economic, social, and environmentally sustained vineyard.

TOP: Sun rising over Bacchus Vineyard showcasing Barrister rows. Winery partners contract for the same rows of grapes year after year.
Photograph by Richard Duval

BELOW: Harvest is finished for the year and the celebration begins with a group photo at Weinbau Vineyard.
Photograph by Kent Waliser

STARS IN A ROW

GOURMET PAIRINGS

Grilled ribeye or braised beef short ribs make perfect companions for this rich wine

TASTING NOTES

The brute strength of Bacchus is tamed by the silky elegance of Dionysus, which offers dried rosemary and thyme from the old Cabernet vines. Rich, dark chocolate from Weinbau's Merlot adds mid-palate texture, plus a hint of dried cherries, and a whiff of cedar box. This bouquet is worth lingering over, and is a worthy lead-in to the layers in each sip.

WINEMAKER'S INSIGHT

The wine is a result of a long-term relationship between Kent Waliser and winemaker, John Abbott of Devona. John has worked with these grapes since 1997 and rightly observes the history of this vineyard. Avoiding the ravages of time and weather has created a powerful experience just being in the vineyard. Kent long dreamt of a Sagemoor Cabernet made from old vine Bacchus fruit.

TECHNICAL DATA

APPELLATION: Columbia Valley
COMPOSITION: 92% Cabernet Sauvignon, 8% Merlot
MATURATION: Aged 18 months in French oak (25% new); matured in bottle for an additional 30 months
CELLARING: Excellent now, peaking around 10 years

ORDER OUR FEATURED WINES

View and order from our collection of outstanding Washington wines

SUCCESSION WINES LAKE CHELAN

"You only live once, but if you do it right, once is enough," Mae West once said. The inspiring words of the inimitable Old Hollywood actress are ones to which Succession Wines owners and founders Erica and Brock Lindsay wholeheartedly subscribe, as they know the beauty of embracing each day and living every moment to the fullest.

Indeed, it is this passion that fuels the couple and acts as a guiding philosophy for them. It's also a philosophy that they were challenged to actually put into practice when two major life events rocked their worlds. In 2014, they welcomed their first child, a daughter, and not two weeks later, they lost their home in the Carlton Complex wildfires.

But, one could say, that it was those two monumental moments that brought them to where they are today—in Washington State, with Succession Wines. Erica and Brock took the good and the bad and used it as an opportunity for replenished strength, significant reflection, and a renewed focus on what is most important in their lives and in their personal journeys. For them, family needed to come first. As they prepared to welcome a second daughter, the love for their growing family and a desire to live a more balanced life—not to mention their passion for great wine—led them back to North Central Washington and their winery was established.

As for the name of their winery, "succession" means the order of things, and it's a term that has special meaning and multidimensional impact for the couple.

FACING PAGE: Acres of award-winning Viognier at Antoine Creek Vineyards, basking in the summer sun, just waiting to be harvested!
Photograph by Erica Lindsay

TOP LEFT: The view from the Tasting Room is nothing short of stunning. Here the sun sets on the mountains and lake as a glass of wine is enjoyed.
Photograph by Brock Lindsay

TOP RIGHT: The Lindsay Family celebrates being named Wine Press Northwest's 2018 winery to watch, a truly distinguished honor.
Photograph by Erica Lindsay

OUR EVOLUTION

GOURMET PAIRINGS

Olive oil and rosemary-marinated pork chops. Accompany them with grilled corn and roasted Brussels sprouts, along with a basil and watermelon salad topped with crumbled feta and balsamic glaze. Perfection!

TASTING NOTES

This is Succession's signature white blend. It is a dry wine with fruit notes of apricot and green apple, accompanied by notes of orange blossom and chamomile. It's textured, well-balanced, vibrant and rich, and finishes with a lovely minerality. Beautiful on its own; it also creates a fantastic pairing with many different foods.

WINEMAKER'S INSIGHT

The grapes for Our Evolution come from the Ancient Lakes AVA. The area is comprised of ancient lava flows that provide unique characteristics in the soil, allowing for the creation of wines with nicely balanced minerality and brightness. Made in stainless steel vats, each wine used in this blend is produced independently and then blended to taste.

AWARDS AND DISTINCTIONS

Double Gold—Wenatchee Food and Wine Festival; Platinum—Wine Press Northwest.

TECHNICAL DATA

APPELLATION: Columbia Valley
COMPOSITION: 67% Semillon, 27% Sauvignon Blanc, 6% Viognier
MATURATION: Aged 6 months in stainless steel tanks.
CELLARING: Enjoy now, or cellar up to three years.

JOIN OUR WINE CLUB

Find out more about our Wine Club by scanning the image on the left

Ecological succession is a term used to describe the process of change in an ecological community over time—often in response to a natural disturbance such as a fire. Fire drastically changed and challenged the lives of Erica and Brock.

Additionally, before he studied the traditional art of winemaking, Brock built bridges. The order of things was critical to his former profession, and it's just as crucial in the winemaking process, too.

Together, with their daughters, they continue to build a new life, a new legacy, and a new succession at their family-friendly (and dog-friendly!) winery overlooking beautiful Lake Chelan.

They are creating their own history, and they invite you to join them on their journey through wine. After all, they truly love seeing others sip, smile, and share stories over a bottle or two of Succession wine.

TOP LEFT: Winemaker, Brock Lindsay, hard at work racking wine.
Photograph by Erica Lindsay

TOP RIGHT: Assistant winemaker, Erica Lindsay, inspecting and tasting wine.
Photograph by Brock Lindsay

ABOVE: Some of our favorite wines! We can't wait to share them with you!!
Photograph by Erica Lindsay

TOP: Barrels get pulled out of the production facility on a sunny day and racked, a critical step in the winemaking process.

LEFT: A little decoration: corks in a glass at the Tasting Room!

ABOVE: Decisions, decisions...which bottle to open?!
Photographs by Erica Lindsay

CABERNET SAUVIGNON

GOURMET PAIRINGS

Porcini-crusted beef tenderloin with a red wine reduction makes for a great pairing. Serve with a side of grilled carrots and wild rice risotto to finish off this meal beautifully.

TASTING NOTES

A concentrated dark fruit of berries and plum greets the palate and melds into smoky black pepper and dark espresso along with leather and humidor. These notes, together with balanced tannins and acidity, create a long smooth finish that lingers and impresses.

WINEMAKER'S INSIGHT

Our Cabernet Sauvignon comes from Antoine Creek Vineyards, a unique growing site on the banks of the Columbia River, in the northern portion of the Columbia Valley AVA. Our grapes are grown on the hottest, highest point of the vineyard on very rocky soil. Antoine Creek sits on an alluvial plain, providing for interesting, exciting wines. The result is a well-balanced Cabernet Sauvignon.

AWARDS & DISTINCTIONS

Double Gold—Wenatchee Food and Wine Festival; Platinum—Wine Press Northwest.

TECHNICAL DATA

APPELLATION: Columbia Valley
COMPOSITION: 100% Cabernet Sauvignon
MATURATION: Aged 20 months in French and Hungarian oak barrels.
CELLARING: Fantastic now, but can be cellared up to 12 years.

LEARN MORE

Learn more about this wine and our winery by scanning the image on the left

TANJULI WINERY ZILLAH

After 25 years of producing wine, Tom Campbell still wasn't ready for retirement. With a deep love for the grapes that hail from the Rattlesnake Hills of the Yakima Valley, it seems Tom has always known crafting wine is his calling. UC Davis classmate—and winemaking partner at both Chateau Ste. Michelle and Quail Run Winery—Stan Clarke introduced Tom to the region in 1981. In 1982, Tom established the white wine production for Quail Run Winery in Zillah, and in 1984, Tom and wife Hema settled in the Rattlesnake Hills to simultaneously start Horizon's Edge Winery and Mission Mountain Winery— the first winery in Montana, Tom's home state. Horizon's Edge, which was founded when fewer than 20 wineries called the region home, was sold in 1999 to allow Tom and Hema to focus on their children and other venture, The Woodhouse Wine Estates in Woodinville. With an undying passion for wine, the couple founded a seven-acre vineyard for the production of authentic estate wines in 2005. As the vines matured, the winery, Tanjuli Winery, was established in 2011.

Named for Tom and Hema's children—Taj and Anjuli—Tanjuli Winery epitomizes the work ethic and resilience of the couple's families. Tradition, heart, and an appreciation for history, as well as Hema's cultural heritage, makes Tanjuli Winery a distinctive destination. Literally nestled into the hillside, the winery itself is surrounded by high-density vineyard. In the cool cellar, natural temperature control from the hillside negates the need for additionally heating and cooling. Visitors appreciate the elegant, simple construction, and lofty floorspace of the winery.

FACING PAGE: Nebbiolo grapes Tanjuli Vineyard.
Photograph by Mike Centioli

ABOVE: The Tanjuli Winery is nestled in the hillside of the Red Peonies.
Photograph by Hema Campbell

Throughout the year, Tanjuli participates in and hosts many events, including special tastings for most major national holidays, the Spring Barrel Tasting, Vertical Estate bottling tastings, Catch the Crush, and Thanksgiving in Wine Country.

As enjoyable as the experience is at the winery, it is the meticulously crafted wines that capture the hearts of aficionados and new wine lovers alike. The Tanjuli vineyard grows Pommard Pinot Noir, Lampia Nebbiolo, Carménère, Mourvèdre, Aglianico, Sagrantino, Teroldego, Viognier, Picpoul Blanc, Orange Muscat, and Black Muscat. Wines are at once old and new, with elements that tickle the imagination yet feel familiar. Rare varietals fascinate the palate while better-known varietals offer a similar, remarkable experience. In addition, they have commenced the process for organic certification.

Throughout the year, Tom and Hema, who is a pharmacist, are hands-on in the vineyard, tending and pruning the vines. At harvest, they're in the vineyards, helping pick grapes. This

deep connection with the land only strengthens the couple's appreciation for all the work needed to craft wine. In the winery, Tom smells the actively fermenting tank or barrel as he creates, on his unfolding adventure to craft even more distinctive wines. Above all, the Campbells appreciate the vivid sensory excitement that comes with drinking wine, how each bottle can evoke memories as you draw the aromas in, and how, when you share a bottle with loved ones, it becomes the foundation of a new memory to cherish for years.

TOP LEFT: Press pan full of Estate Carménère.
Photograph by Tom Campbell

BELOW LEFT: Guests congregating and sampling wines in our tasting room is a common occurance at Tanjuli Winery.
Photograph by Raj Shah

ABOVE: Hema Campbell can be often seen around the winery, here topping barrels of a latest vintage.
Photograph by Tom Campbell

ESTATE CARMÉNÈRE

GOURMET PAIRINGS

Our Estate Carménère pairs well with thick-cut lamb chops, seasoned with crushed black pepper and kosher salt, fire-grilled to medium rare.

TASTING NOTES

A nose of blackberry and black currant among herbal hints of thyme and eucalyptus with black and white peppercorns distinguishes the Estate Carménère. The pour brings flavors of cassis, boysenberry, and pomegranate—a fruity mix that makes for juicy acidity and medium tannins, backed by a slice of red bell pepper.

WINEMAKER'S INSIGHT

Carménère is one of the most ancient European varieties being brought back from extinction by wineries in the New World, like ours. There have been suggestions that Carménère may be Biturica, a vine praised in Ancient Rome and also the name by which the city of Boudreaux was known during that era. The high-density planting and extensive crop thinning allow us to achieve the concentration of flavor in this wine. With some patience and attention to detail in the winemaking process, the consumer receives quality they instantly recognize. Time, care, and a sense of place are required to give this authentic experience. That is the magic of Tanjuli Winery.

AWARDS AND DISTINCTIONS

Rated Outstanding – Great Northwest Wine

TECHNICAL DATA

APPELLATION: Yakima Valley
COMPOSITION: 100% Carménère
MATURATION: Aged 2 years in selected oak barrels then bottle-aged a year before release
CELLARING: Great now and able to age for an additional 15 years if stored properly

LEARN MORE

Visit our wine store by scanning the image to left

TAPTEIL VINEYARD WINERY BENTON CITY

Early experiences visiting wineries and vineyards in Australia, Washington, Oregon, and California, left Tapteil Vineyard Winery founder Larry Pearson with lasting impressions of the beauty of those agricultural areas and the personal connection people have with wine. In the early 1980s, he found himself back in Seattle continuing his engineering consultant career, and with the capability to realistically search for land upon which to build a vineyard. During his search, he looked for the perfect site for growing Cabernet Sauvignon. Serendipitously, he found that site on Red Mountain during his search, and along the way, his expanding appreciation for Washington State grapes provided further inspiration in establishing his vineyard.

While searching for the perfect place to establish a vineyard and winery, Larry also searched for the perfect name. His search led him to the Library of Congress in Washington, DC. There, he researched historical documents about the early explorers and missionaries who documented early interactions with the Native Americans living in the area. From these, he found the terms "Tapteil" and "Tapteilmin," which refer to the Yakima River and the people who called the river valley home. "Tapteil" comes from the Sahaptin language of the Yakama and Nez Perce peoples who inhabited this region of the Pacific Northwest. The word directly translates to "narrow," and refers to the narrow portion of the Yakima River as it flows to the Columbia River.

On land that was previously used for grazing, Tapteil Vineyard was first planted in 1985. Although not the first vineyard on Red Mountain, it was

FACING PAGE: The front of Tapteil Vineyard Winery featuring the logo "Earth, Wind, and Water."

ABOVE: A sweeping panoramic view of the Red Mountain AVA and the Yakima Valley from the terrace at Tapteil. *Photographs by Richard Duvall*

among the earliest in the area. To Larry's delight, the Red Mountain American Viticultural Area was approved in 2001, 16 years after the start of his vineyard, and added more validation that Red Mountain was an exceptional area for producing wine. In the early days, friends and family were recruited to help, and much of the work was done by hand to plant and harvest the grapes. The only building on the site at that time was the pump house—the ever-important water source. But with a love of what the vineyard could offer, Larry began building his dream. Today, Tapteil Vineyard is planted to Cabernet Sauvignon, Cabernet Franc, Merlot, Malbec, Petit Verdot, Syrah, Grenache, and Mourvedre. There's also a block of Riesling planted at the edge of the Yakima River. The latest plantings at the Badlands include more Cabernet Sauvignon as well as the Italian varietal, Aglianico.

TOP: Larry and Jane Pearson enjoying a glass of wine in the Tapteil Vineyard on the slope of Red Mountain.

LEFT: Our signature wines on display at the Tapteil tasting room. *Photographs by Noah Forbes*

ARTIST SERIES SYRAH

GOURMET PAIRINGS

Pairs well with grilled sausage and peppers, or grilled lamb burgers on grilled bread, brushed with olive oil on a bed of greens, topped with tzatziki

TASTING NOTES

Syrah grapes were sourced from the Spilya Vineyard block of Tapteil Vineyard planted in 2002. The Artist Series Syrah is a blend of two clones, Phelps and SaraLee. This rich, dark wine exhibits nuances of spice, blackberry, marionberry, with dry tobacco and chocolate notes. Tannins are fine-grained and provide a complete palate to go with a range of flavorful grilled dishes.

WINEMAKER'S INSIGHT

Syrah grapes were picked mid-September based upon brix, pH, and acidity, destemmed with minimal crushing, dropped by gravity into one-ton bins, cold-soaked for 48 hours, then inoculated with selected wine yeasts, hand punched down twice daily, and transferred to barrels where the wine finishes both primary and secondary fermentation.

AWARDS AND DISTINCTIONS

Double Gold – Seattle Wine Awards

TECHNICAL DATA

APPELLATION: Yakima Valley

COMPOSITION: 100% Syrah, two clones: Phelps and SaraLee

MATURATION: 21 months in American, French, and Hungarian oak, 20% new

CELLARING: Enjoyable soon after bottling, but always best after one year and can be cellared for four to six years

VISIT OUR STORE

Enter our store by scanning image on left. or visit www.tapteil.com/our-wines/

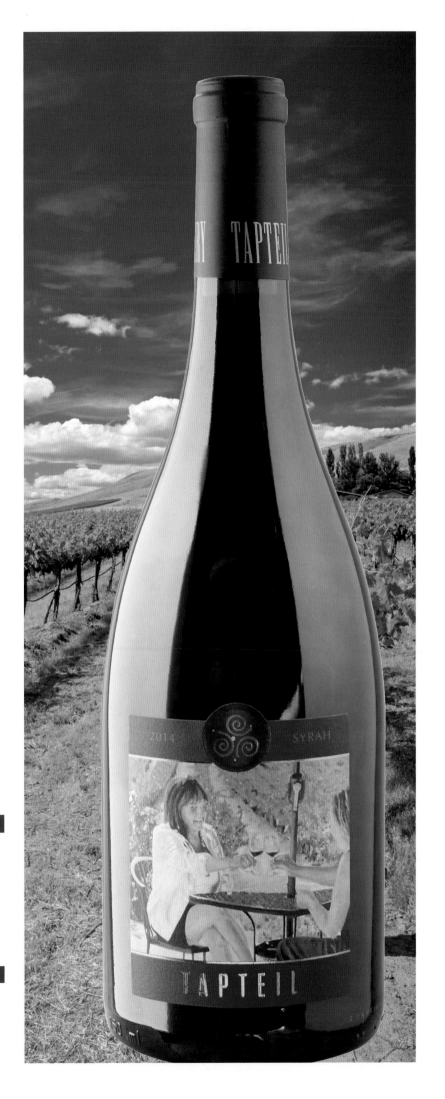

CABERNET SAUVIGNON

GOURMET PAIRINGS
Delicious with slow-roasted standing rib roast with baked potatoes for special occasions, or grilled lamb popsicles with boiled new potatoes and asparagus.

TASTING NOTES
Cabernet Sauvignon grapes were sourced from the original Tapteil Vineyard block planted in 1985. The wine exhibits nuances of dusty spice, dark cherry, and currant with cocoa powder and plum. Tannins are fine-grained and firm. The Tapteil Cabernet Sauvignon is powerful and full-bodied with ripe and rich flavors and a complete palate which shows the length, complexity, and balance of these Red Mountain-grown grapes.

WINEMAKER'S INSIGHT
Cabernet Sauvignon grapes picked mid to late-September based upon the brix, pH, and acidity, destemmed with minimal crushing, dropped by gravity into 1-ton bins, cold-soaked for 48 hours, then inoculated with selected wine yeast, hand punched down twice daily and transferred to barrels where the wine finished both primary and secondary fermentation.

AWARDS AND DISTINCTIONS
Double Gold – Seattle Wine Awards
Gold – Great Northwest Invitational Wine Competition

TECHNICAL DATA

APPELLATION: Red Mountain
COMPOSITION: 100% Cabernet Sauvignon
MATURATION: 21 months in French oak, 80% new
CELLARING: Can be enjoyed two months after bottling, but cellaring for six to eight years can provide additional enjoyment

BUY THIS WINE

Buy this wine and more by scanning the image on the left or visit www.tapteil.com/our-wines/

The vineyard has become a gathering place for a family and friends, and just as he did in the early days, Larry welcomes visitors to the vineyard—by appointment these days—and the tasting room throughout the year. In 2001, Larry met his future wife, Jane, and they were married in 2004. She serves as the marketing director and focuses on marketing, sales, the wine club, and tasting room operations. Jane is also the artist who provides the work for the winery's Artist Series Syrah. In the vineyard, Genaro Cazares, in the winery, Kenneth Corliss, and in the tasting room Gayle Garvie, Wendy Davis, and Talia Ochoa assist the Pearsons with day-to-day operations. Each year, the winery hosts public events including the Red Wine & Chocolate event in mid-February, the Spring Barrel Tasting in April, Catch the Crush in late-September and mid-October, and Thanksgiving in Wine Country on Thanksgiving weekend, in addition to two annual wine club events.

TOP: Tapteil's new vineyard at the Badlands with the Yakima River and Red Mountain in the background.
Photograph by Richard Duvall

BELOW LEFT & RIGHT: Argus and Hugo serve as Director of First Impressions and Official Greeter.
Photographs by Noah Forbes

TSILLAN CELLARS WINERY LAKE CHELAN

Named for 55-mile-long Lake Chelan, which it overlooks, Tsillan Cellars Winery and Vineyards—pronounced "Chelan"—is the brainchild of Dr. Bob Jankelson, who saw the potential for vinifera grapes when the apple industry faltered in the late 1990s. Dr. Jankelson researched the growing history of the region and soon confirmed his hunch that grapes would thrive on the south shore of Lake Chelan. So, he purchased 40 prime orchard acres in 2000 and began planting vinifera varieties in 2001. An additional 90 acres was purchased in 2003. He named the vineyard and winery Tsillan Cellars as a nod to the history of the region—"tsillan" is a Native American word for deep water and was the word that described the area in the original survey dating back to 1826.

With reverence for local heritage, Dr. Jankelson was also inspired by Italian culture and architecture from his career teaching around the globe. That inspiration is evident in Tsillan Cellars Winery and Sorrento's Ristorante. Stunning Italian-style bell towers, a clock tower, columns, and 80,000 pounds of Italian marble and stone greet visitors as they drive up the vineyard-lined entrance. Sorrento's Ristorante, clad in glass, opens to the outdoors with spectacular al fresco dining in the warm summer months that seems to reinforce the feeling that you've been transported to Tuscany. Spectacular waterfalls, gardens, and terrazzos invite guests to enjoy Tsillan Cellars estate wines surrounded by the natural beauty of Lake Chelan.

Since the initial plantings in 2001 of Riesling, Pinot Grigio, Gewurztraminer, Syrah, Merlot, and Malbec, the vineyard has expanded to also include

FACING PAGE: The Upper Terrazzo features a koi pond which overlooks the entire winery.
Photograph courtesy of Tsillan Cellars Winery

ABOVE: Enter the tasting room and make your way to the Italian marble countertop to enjoy a wine tasting.
Photograph by Bella Fritz Photography

213

ESTATE MALBEC

GOURMET PAIRINGS

The rounded red fruit and color seen in the complexity of our Malbec make it a wonderful pairing with your favorite red meat dish, like grilled mushroom burgers, ribeye steaks, and pot roast.

TASTING NOTES

The Malbec is deep and rich in color with a wonderful round nose of mint, black currant, and vanilla aromas. The silky-smooth elegance brings an enjoyable consistency to the wine. It's full-bodied and full of flavors including boysenberry syrup, overripe cherries, and roasted chestnuts.

WINEMAKER'S INSIGHT

With the heat units of our AVA regularly reaching over 3,000 growing degree days, it results in a bold expression of ripe fruit. The wines made from this varietal are some of our most awarded. All of the fermentation takes place in one-ton stainless-steel bins where it is then pressed off into tanks before being sent off to barrel.

AWARDS AND DISTINCTIONS

Best of Category – 2017 Northwest Wine Summit;
Gold Medal – Northwest Wine Summit, Seattle Wine Awards, West Coast Wine Competition

TECHNICAL DATA

APPELLATION: Lake Chelan
COMPOSITION: 100% Malbec
MATURATION: Aged 20 months in oak barrels. About 60% allotted to new oak barrels and 40% to neutral barrels
CELLARING: Great potential for cellaring for up to eight to 10 years, but also ready to drink upon release

LEARN MORE

Learn more about Tsillan Cellars wines by scanning image on the left

TOP: A look at Tsillan Cellars estate vineyard surrounding the winery.

ABOVE: The outstanding view of Tsillan Cellars winery and vineyards overlooking Lake Chelan.
Photographs by Bella Fritz Photography

Cabernet Sauvignon, Sangiovese, Barbera, Dolcetto, Grenache, and Cabernet Franc. Presently, Tsillan Cellars is entirely an estate winery, using only fruit from its lush, unique vineyards. Critics and connoisseurs have taken notice—several bottlings have received Gold and Double Gold Medals from competitions, including the Indy International Wine Competition, the Seattle Wine Awards, the Wine Press NW Platinum Judging, and the Cascadia Wine Competition. In all, the winery has amassed over 400 gold and platinum awards, but it is the people as well as the exceptional wine that brings guests back to Tsillan Cellars time and again.

Dr. Jankelson will introduce himself as Bob when he runs into you at the winery, and is always ready to chat about his philosophy and vision for winemaking. A self-professed "romantic," he embraces the small things in life and cherishes interactions with visitors. General Manager Dave Moore ensures everything runs in tip-top shape, and coordinates all aspects of the hospitality operations. Ray Sandidge, head winemaker, has more than 30 years of winemaking experience to his name in Europe and North America, and is assisted by Devon Griffith. Together, the pair ensures the winemaking process remains consistent and exceptional.

Other key members of the operation include Bal Flores, who has been the vineyard manager for 14 years; Carrie McGuinn, who serves as Wine Club manager and office administrator; and Ashtyn Mann, who manages the tasting room operations. Jamie Dowell, marketing director, Cassy Schlunegar, assistant Wine Club manager, and Alexa Hammond, who manages the Tsillan Cellars Woodinville tasting room, further ensure guests and consumers experience the best of what Tsillan Cellars has to offer. At Sorrento's, Executive Chef Brian Ensminger and Executive Banquet Chef Brett Rayment craft Italian cuisine that's bar none.

Throughout the year, guests are invited to attend public events including Red Wine and Chocolate, Lake Chelan Spring Release, Spring Barrel Tasting, Lake Chelan Crush, and Fall Barrel Tasting. The winery's breathtaking views are also perfect for weddings and special events catered by Sorrento's. Wine Club members experience even more events and enjoy exclusive privileges that are too good to pass up.

TOP LEFT: A grape vine covered trellis runs above a natural slate terrazzo. The perfect place to enjoy the serenity of the winery.

RIGHT: The winery features a 35-foot bell tower with a 650 lb bronze bell. Make sure to give it a ring when you go inside!

TOP: From soil to glass, every step of the aging process is done on the estate. *Photographs by Bella Fritz Photography*

ESTATE RIESLING

GOURMET PAIRINGS

The sleeper of wines in the food pairing world, our Estate Riesling's strong backbone of lively acidity makes it a great accompaniment to salads, soups, chicken, beef, or pork entrees.

TASTING NOTES

Our Estate Riesling is a bright green straw color, with aromas of honey, applesauce, and citrus blossoms. On the palate, bright citrus components give the wine a lively acidity with subtle, sweet notes of round stone fruit, including apricot and peach. The balance of residual sugar and acidity makes it an ideal food pairing wine.

WINEMAKER'S INSIGHT

The vineyard shift we experience here on the estate from the influence of the lake not only protects the wines from winter damage but also helps maintain the acidity of the varietals such as Riesling. Each lot is handpicked, sorted, and pressed as whole clusters.

AWARDS AND DISTINCTIONS

Double Gold Medal – Indy International Wine Competition, Seattle Wine Awards
Gold Medals – West Coast Wine Competition, Los Angeles International Wine Competition, Seattle Wine Awards

TECHNICAL DATA

APPELLATION: Lake Chelan
COMPOSITION: 100% Riesling
MATURATION: After fermentation, it is left to cold settle for four and half months
CELLARING: Ready to enjoy upon release but holds incredible aging potential with its high acid content

LEARN MORE

Visit our wine store by scanning the image to left

VanArnam Vineyards ZILLAH

On nearly 40 acres of rolling land sits VanArnam Vineyards, a winery where the intimate relationship between the vineyard and the wine produced from it is epitomized. Owners Kent and Allison VanArnam grew up in California and were exposed, firsthand, to some of the oldest vineyards and wineries in the nation. When they moved to Washington State, they quickly realized just how special the Yakima Valley is for growing wine grapes. With the understanding that exquisite wine comes from exceptional vineyards, the couple took the next several years to meticulously search for the perfect place to establish their winery. In 2007, they found it: 40 acres of southwest-facing land with soil well-suited for growing grapes, with the right level of organic mass and water drainage. Much to the delight of all who visit, the vineyards also enjoy the captivating views of Mt. Adams and Mt. Rainier. The VanArnams joke that the grapes grow so well because they appreciate the view as much as everyone else.

As owners and active managers of the winery, Kent and Allison can often be found in the vineyard or the winery. Their children, Paige and Max, helped the pair plant and build everything one sees at VanArnam Vineyards, and on a typical weekend, it's common to find Allison in the tasting room and Kent out on his tractor among the vines. The careful stewardship with which the VanArnams care for the land—and the heart and soul they pour into winemaking—makes VanArnam Vineyards wines so appealing. The vines are pruned by hand to guide each to their optimum potential.

LEFT Owners, Kent and Allison VanArnam in front of the cedar winery door Kent built by hand.

ABOVE LEFT: VanArnam Vineyards Tasting Room in Zillah, Washington, during one of our beautiful sunsets.

ABOVE RIGHT: Vistors enjoy a view of Mt. Adams from the tasting room patio.
Photographs courtesy of VanArnam Vineyards

During harvest, each cluster is also picked by hand. After fermentation in small fermenters, each wine is drained straight from the fermenting bins—called free run—and gives the wine a smooth palate without harsh tannins. While the winemaking team may sometimes add a bit of lightly-pressed wine to a vintage for fuller mouthfeel, the focus is on creating exceptionally high-quality, free-run wine. Wine critics and fans of VanArnam Vineyards agree—the choice to specialize in free run wine makes the winery's offerings something truly special.

Whether you want to sample VanArnam Vineyards' bold Cabernet Sauvignon, or the Syrah, Merlot, Malbec, or Cabernet Franc, a visit to the winery is nothing short of magical. Throughout the year, the wine, the views, and events draw visitors to the sloping vineyards and Tuscan-inspired winery: Red Wine and Chocolate, the Spring Barrel Tasting, Catch the Crush, and Thanksgiving in Wine Country.

TOP: We couldn't be more pleased than seeing our tasting room guests enjoying our wine.

BELOW LEFT: River, the winery dog taking a break from her job of greeting the guests.

BELOW LEFT: The VanArnam family; Max VanArnam, Paige VanArnam, Allison VanArnam, and Kent VanArnam.
Photographs courtesy of VanArnam Vineyards

ESTATE RESERVE CABERNET

GOURMET PAIRINGS

Our bold Reserve Cabernet complements the roast meat of beef tagliata well, and stands up to the intense flavors of radicchio and arugula salad with a sharp flavor of Parmesan cheese.

TASTING NOTES

The estate-grown Cabernet Sauvignon is made from free-run juice. Twenty-two months in French barrels leads to aromas of toasted marshmallow, fresh-pulled espresso, cherries, and black tea, followed by flavors of Chukar Cherries, dark plums, and caramel. Focused chocolaty tannins with a hint of toasted almond make for an elegant finish.

WINEMAKER'S INSIGHT

Our winemaking starts in the vineyard where long warm and dry summers allow plenty of time for the grapes to fully ripen with strong sugars, and cool nights keep the acids strong for a well-balanced fruit upon harvest. Hand-harvested clusters are fermented in small bins. After fermentation, the free run juice is separated before pressing. Our wines are made from primarily free-run juice to display the full flavor of the fruit with mild tannins. Depending on the vintage, we may blend in some lightly-pressed wine to add depth for a fuller mouthfeel.

AWARDS & DISTINCTIONS

First place – SIP Northwest Wine Competition in Seattle

TECHNICAL DATA

APPELLATION: Yakima Valley
COMPOSITION: 100% Cabernet Sauvignon
MATURATION: Aged 22 months in French oak
CELLARING: Exquisite upon release but can be cellared for up to 10 years

LEARN MORE

Visit our website by scanning the imageon the left

BELOW: Walla Walla Valley vineyards in the Mill Creek growing area overlooking the base of the Blue Mountains.

FACING PAGE TOP LEFT: Guests enjoying a vintage wine tasting as part of the annual "Celebrate Walla Walla Valley Wine" events.

FACING PAGE TOP RIGHT: Visitors take-in the views while mingling with Justin Wylie, owner and winemaker of Va Piano Vineyards.

FACING PAGE BOTTOM: Preparing for an intimate collaborative winemaker dinner at Tranche, along with Walla Walla Vintners and Aluvé Winery.
Photographs courtesy of WWVWA/Duval Images

WALLA WALLA VALLEY

Presented by The Walla Walla Valley Wine Alliance

Located in a beautiful valley amid the vast sagebrush desert, the Walla Walla Valley boasts a heritage of exceptional agriculture. For over a century, the lush region, whose name means "many waters," has been a premier source of delicious produce, including exquisite wine grapes. On February 2, 1984, the region officially gained recognition for its grapes, with the establishment of the Walla Walla Valley America Viticultural Area (AVA). It is the state's second oldest AVA, after Yakima Valley. In just over three decades, the region has emerged as one of the must-see wine destinations in the world for both its palate-captivating wines and the people who make it special. Camaraderie and forward-thinking are ingrained in the Walla Walla Valley wine industry. Winemakers constantly support one another, whether the wine is made out of garages or from one of the landmark wineries that has been there from the beginning.

At latitude 46°N, Longitude 118.5°W, the AVA shares a latitude with French wine country—the 46°N point lies midway between Bordeaux and Burgundy. That similarity is reflected in the rich red wine grapes that grow so prolifically in the region, namely Cabernet Sauvignon, Merlot, Syrah, and Cabernet Franc. Over 3,000 acres of planted vineyards span the AVA from southeastern Washington to northeastern Oregon. Elevations soar from 400 feet to 2,000 feet above sea level, and annual rainfall figures triple across the appellation, from seven inches in the western section to 22 inches per year in the foothills of the Blue Mountains to the east.

At the heart of the valley is historic downtown Walla Walla. Its diverse art scene and exceptional outdoor experiences complement its popular restaurants, boutique shops, neighborhood cafés, and of course, local tasting rooms. When you arrive, you'll immediately feel at home. Don't be surprised if a local winemaker, dressed in jeans and boots, strikes up a conversation at a local café or a stranger greets you with a hello in this charming region.

AMAVI CELLARS   WALLA WALLA

Wineries often start with an individual's passion for wine. At Amavi Cellars, the love of wine and the passion for life are apparent. From the Zen-like Walla Walla tasting room to the very name itself—Amavi represents love, "amor," and life, "vita"—everything about the winery is focused on the experience of enjoying wine. Founded by Pepper Bridge Winery's same three families, the Goffs, Pellets, and McKibbens, Amavi Cellars' first vintage was 2001, released in 2003. As members of the Walla Walla Valley Wine Alliance, the Amavi Cellars family views winemaking as a lifestyle, working for the growth of the region and showcasing the unique qualities of the Walla Walla Valley.

The winery prides itself on 100 percent estate grown fruit, 100 percent sustainability, and being 100 percent Walla Walla. Amavi Cellars wines are made from grapes grown in six vineyards: Pepper Bridge, Les Collines, Seven Hills, Octave, Summit View, and Goff, and the focus is on crafting exceptional wine while preserving the environment. Dedicated to responsible stewardship and committed to leaving the land better for future generations, the Amavi Cellars team prioritizes the balance between environmental, economic, and social factors involved in the process of growing grapes and producing wine. Part of that mission of sustainability means that Amavi Cellars has, since the beginning, sourced grapes only from the Walla Walla Valley. Eric McKibben, General Manager, and siblings are second generation partners in the winery and share the same family philosophy and lifestyle.

FACING PAGE: The patio of the Amavi Cellars tasting room in Walla Walla allows guests to enjoy an inspiring view of the vineyard and the Blue Mountains.
Photograph by Jack von Eberstein

TOP LEFT: Amavi Cellars' vintage Chevy truck against a beautiful Walla Walla sunset in the Pepper Bridge Vineyard.
Photograph by Wilton Photography

TOP RIGHT: Amavi Cellars' block in the Seven Hills Vineyard.
Photograph by Rose Pingree

AMAVI CELLARS CABERNET SAUVIGNON

GOURMET PAIRINGS
Pairs well with steak, cassoulet, and grilled Portobello mushrooms.

TASTING NOTES
Raspberry, black cherry, baking spices, and vanilla bean tickle the nose of this lush Cabernet Sauvignon. With flavors or blackberry compote and toasted hazelnuts, the wine features a rich mid-palate and a velvety tannin structure.

WINEMAKER'S INSIGHT
Within all our vineyards, we dedicate ourselves to being stewards of the land. Warm days and cool nights allow for the perfect development of Amavi Cellars' trademark acidity. Beautifully structured, ripe, and expressive, the Cabernet Sauvignon pairs well with hearty dishes or is excellent enjoyed alone. Praise from Paul Gregutt: "Clearly one of Walla Walla's value superstars."

AWARDS & DISTINCTIONS
Top 100 Wine – Wine Spectator
Winemaker of the Year – Washington Wine Awards

TECHNICAL DATA

APPELLATION: Walla Walla Valley
COMPOSITION: Cabernet Sauvignon, Cabernet Franc, Merlot, Malbec
MATURATION: Aged approximately 17 months in mostly neutral barrels; 96% French oak and 4% American oak
CELLARING: Delicious upon release and ages very gracefully for years to come

ORDER OUR WINES

Enter our store by scanning image on left or visit www.amavicellars.orderport.net/wines/

The winery features two tasting rooms, one in Walla Walla and the second in Woodinville, where guests can learn about the winemaking process, schedule private tastings, and sample some of Amavi Cellars' current offerings. The winery's collection of Syrah, Cabernet Sauvignon, Semillon, and Cabernet Franc Rosé, are ready to drink upon release and age well for serious collectors. Not only are the wines pleasing to the palate, but they're also a great value. Wine Spectator, The Rhone Report, and Wine & Spirits Magazine have sung Amavi Cellars' praises as a top winery with a fantastic value, and the Sommelier Journal has said that Amavi will "Drive red Rhone lovers gaga." With such high praise, it's no wonder guests flock to the tasting rooms and immediately fall in love.

TOP: The view framing the stunning Blue Mountains from the Walla Walla tasting room.
Photograph by Jack von Eberstein

RIGHT: Ray Goff, Managing Partner, and Jean-François Pellet, Winemaker/Partner in the barrel room.
Photograph by Amy Allen Photography

BASEL CELLARS ESTATE WINERY

The enchantment in every bottle of Basel Cellars Estate Winery's wine–be it red, white, or rosé–is undeniable. The richness of deep fruit; the distinction of Columbia Valley character and Walla Walla dirt; the depth of full-bodied flavors with smooth tannins and supple texture—there's really nothing that doesn't entice and delight.

So, it's no surprise that such high-caliber, inspiring wines hail from an equally enchanting estate; an estate that makes Basel Cellars the premier destination winery in Walla Walla.

Founded in 2002, Basel Cellars was born when local grape grower Greg Basel purchased a 96-acre estate formerly known as Double River Ranch. The site had three vital components to creating a successful winery. First: The environment. Rich soil and a hilltop location between Yellowhawk Creek and the Walla Walla River were the perfect conditions for the 29 acres of vineyards that would be planted. Secondly, the grandeur of the 14,000-square-foot, lodge-style house on the property—not to mention its 2,000-square-foot poolside cabana—couldn't have been more ideal for transforming the ranch into a magnificent tasting room and event venue. And, third: The property's 9,600-square-foot, temperature-controlled, subterranean structure, which had previously housed a car collection, was tailor-made for winemaking—just like the caves of France! Affectionately called the "bat cave" by the Basel Cellars team, this underground space is where all of their wine is produced.

FACING PAGE: Guests who visit Basel Cellars Estate Winery & Resort are treated to scenic views of the estates 29 acres of vineyards.

TOP: The entrance to the estate property and vineyard is as grand as the tasting room and resort house itself.
Photographs by Mark Myers

MERRIMENT

GOURMET PAIRINGS

Braised and grilled Wagyu short ribs with Walla Walla sweet onion and balsamic jam, Yukon potatoes, and roasted Brussels sprouts, seared in bacon fat with black pepper.

TASTING NOTES

The expressive aroma shows prominent hints of leather, cedar, and black currant. As this wine breathes, you will be rewarded with noticeable nuances of violets, fruitcake, dark chocolate, and dried sage. Ripe, dark fruit flavors are very noticeable in the mouthfeel, where notes of cherry and blackberry marry beautifully with ample tannin and warm oak tones.

WINEMAKER'S INSIGHT

Our Merriment is comprised of our best vineyard blocks from a specific vintage. The most balanced and elegant barrels from these lots gets selected for this Bordeaux-style blend. Only the best French oak is used for these specific blocks and it matures for about 20 months in barrel. The unique terroir of each of these vineyards bring its own identity to this wine.

AWARDS AND DISTINCTIONS

91 points, Stephen Tanzer

TECHNICAL DATA

APPELLATION: Columbia Valley
COMPOSITION: 50% Cabernet Sauvignon, 18% Malbec, 18% Cabernet Franc, 14% Merlot
MATURATION: Aged 20 months in 100% French oak barrels
CELLARING: Can be cellared for up to 10 to 15 years

VISIT OUR STORE

Buy this wine by scanning image on left

TOP: The Basel Cellars tasting room in Walla Walla, overlooks the estate vineyard, providing picturesque views of the Blue Mountains.
Photograph by Mark Myers

MIDDLE: The 14,000 square foot estate house and tasting room and the 9,600 square foot underground temperature controlled cellar are unique features of the winery
Photograph by Ali Walker

BOTTOM: Guests who rent the estate house can enjoy these views of the vineyard from the outdoor patio at all times of the day.
Photograph by Mark Myers

In 2004, Greg invited Steve and Jo Marie Hansen, acquaintances from earlier careers, to visit Basel Cellars and experience the still-young operation with an eye towards becoming partners in the future. As it turns out, it proved to be a good match. Steve, a long-time construction manager of major bridge and highway projects in the western US, grew up in a farming family in Yakima, Washington. He not only brought an entrepreneurial spirit with him, but also a love for the land and the sunny side of the state. The couple began their partnership with a fifty percent ownership of the winery.

Seven years later, Steve and Jo Marie began transitioning into full ownership of Basel Cellars Estate Winery.

And, their team now also includes wine grower and general manager Ryan Sams and winemaker Dirk Brink. Above and beyond relishing the beautiful wines that are produced, Steve and Jo Marie find so much joy in meeting each and every guest who comes to Basel Cellars and sharing the beautiful winery experience that captivated them since their first weekend visit there in 2004.

Basel Cellars has three tasting rooms, having added Woodinville and Leavenworth locations to the mix along with the original Walla Walla estate, where wine lovers can sample the full portfolio including Sauvignon Blanc Semillon, Cabernet Sauvignon, Cabernet Franc, Claret, Merlot, Malbec, Carmenere, and Syrah.

But, if you ask Steve and Jo Marie, the most superior tasting opportunity is really at Walla Walla—it's the true expression of a wine country escape, where guests can even stay overnight at the estate and fully experience its lush surrounds that feature the majestic house along with a pool, hot tub, private movie theater, and multiple outdoor barbecues and patios.

Basel Cellars Estate Winery not only hosts getaways for friends and families, but also private events, corporate retreats, weddings, and more. It's a chance to live like royalty for a few days—and drink like a king or queen, too.

TOP: The 14,000 square foot home is perfect for family getaways, trips with friends, private events, corporate retreats, weddings and more.
Photographs by Mark Meyers

BELOW LEFT: Owners Jo Marie and Steve Hansen became 50 percent owners of Basel Cellars in 2004, and transitioned to full ownership in 2011.
Photographs by Ali Walker

DOUBLE RIVER ESTATE
CABERNET SAUVIGNON

GOURMET PAIRINGS

Sous vide New York strip steak with slow-cooked pork belly, Walla Walla Valley butternut squash, and lollipop kale, all covered with a vibrant, black-cherry demi glaze.

TASTING NOTES

This wine exhibits an expressive fragrance of ripe cherry, black currant, and licorice. It is floral, yet earthy, showcasing hints of lavender, red root vegetables, wet stone, and dry leaves. It is well-structured in the mid-palate, with an intensity of red fruit lingering between multiple layers of oak, fleshy tannin, and fair acidity.

WINEMAKER'S INSIGHT

We select the best block of Cabernet Sauvignon for this estate bottling. The diversity of Block 9 and its distinct terroir deliver exciting and strong nuances in this exclusive offering of Cabernet Sauvignon. Small, ripe, and intense berries are handled with special care in the cellar to reveal the unique flavor profile of this particular block.

AWARDS AND DISTINCTIONS

90 points – Stephen Tanzer

TECHNICAL DATA

APPELLATION: Walla Walla Valley
COMPOSITION: 100% Cabernet Sauvignon
MATURATION: Aged 22 months in 100% French oak barrels
CELLARING: Can be cellared for up to 10 to 12 years

LEARN MORE

Learn more about this wine and our winery by scanning the image on the left

DOUBLE RIVER ESTATE SYRAH

GOURMET PAIRINGS

Upper Dry Creek lamb chops with Blue Mountain morel risotto, fresh frog hollow beets, and Rea Farms English peas.

TASTING NOTES

This Syrah shows vivid aromas of blueberry, dark chocolate, and accents of cherry on the nose. Definite nuances of orange peel, rose petal, and lavender bring brightness and finesse to this wine. Warm, subtle oak tones along with savory hints of bacon create more intensity and depth on the bouquet. The round and pleasant mouthfeel delivers dark berry fruits, great acidity, and mature tannins.

WINEMAKER'S INSIGHT

This wine is crafted from Block 8 at our Double River Estate Vineyard. With a modest and hands-off approach in the cellar—respecting the fruit and terroir—we give this wine the freedom to develop its own distinct identity. It is slowly fermented in small batches, then aged in French oak for about 18 months.

AWARDS AND DISTINCTIONS

93 points – Wine Spectator

TECHNICAL DATA

APPELLATION: Walla Walla Valley
COMPOSITION: 100% Syrah
MATURATION: Aged 18 months in 100% French oak barrels
CELLARING: Can be cellared for up to 10 years

VISIT OUR STORE

Buy this wine by scanning image on left

TOP: The tasting room was originally built to serve as a garage for the personal residence.
Photograph by Mark Myers

ABOVE: Basel Cellars Winemaker Dirk Brink visits with guests of the estate house as they sample wines in the tasting room
Photograph by Mark Myers

RIGHT: Ryan Sams serves as Basel Cellars wine grower and general manager.
Photograph by Ali Walker

BROWNE FAMILY VINEYARDS WALLA WALLA

Browne Family Vineyards was 15 years in the making before its first vintage ever debuted. Andrew Browne, principal of Browne Family Vineyards, carefully curated the best talent and top vineyards to realize his dream of world-class wine production. Inspired by the greatness of one man—Andrew's late grandfather, William Bitner Browne—integrity and excellence are the standards upon which Browne wines were created.

Browne Family Vineyards has the luxury of land. With fruit sourced from the best estate vineyards throughout Washington's Columbia Valley, winemaker John Freeman crafts outstanding Bordeaux-inspired reds and full-bodied whites aged extensively in French oak. With over twenty 90-plus scores, the wines represent a commitment to uncompromised quality.

Relationships are the cornerstone of Browne Family Vineyards, with each wine dedicated to a member of Andrew's family. Visitors to the Browne Family tasting room in downtown Walla Walla or in Seattle's historic Pioneer Square are made to feel like family, sharing in a long-time tradition of enjoying fine wines in good company.

LEFT Proprietor Andrew Browne, with his daughter, Ellie, viewing a photo of his grandfather and winery inspiration, William Bitner Browne.

ABOVE RIGHT Proprietor Andrew Browne, Winemaker John Freeman, and Viticulturalist Dave Minick at Browne Family Estate Vineyard, Spring Valley District, Walla Walla AVA.

ABOVE LEFT: Enjoy many acclaimed wines, such as our Tribute Red Blend, at our Walla Walla tasting room.
Photographs courtesy of Browne Family Vineyards

CADERETTA WINERY WALLA WALLA

A blend of science and soul, tempered with tradition and balance, Cadaretta Winery makes wines that are as multidimensional and distinctive as its history. Founded and owned by the Middleton family, who have deep roots of 120 years in Washington's timber industry, Cadaretta is actually named for a lumber schooner that once carried their goods to market up and down the Pacific Coast in the early part of the 20th century. Southwind, their estate vineyard, is named for the same ship, which was rechristened when it served in World War II.

Of course, the story doesn't stop at logs and lumber. The Middletons began farming grapes in the mid '90s, adding winemaking skill and experience to their longstanding agricultural heritage in Washington. In 2005, they brought their grape and wine experience to the Walla Walla area with Cadaretta, thus joining their essential commitment to the land with an abiding passion for making the best wine from that land.

The first vines of the Southwind Vineyard were planted in 2007. Located on a steep slope with the highest altitude point of 1,431 feet, the vineyard features both ancient soils above the Missoula flood line as well as more typical soils of the Columbia Valley. Putting the benefits of both soil profiles to use, Cadaretta produces red varietals including Cabernet Sauvignon, Syrah, and Malbec, along with several red blends in the Bordeaux and Rhône styles. Their singular white wine is a Sauvignon Blanc-Semillon blend named "SBS."

FACING PAGE: The Glasshouse sits atop our Southwind Vineyard and looks out over the Walla Walla Valley. Open for invitation only tastings and events.

TOP LEFT: Cadaretta Barrels.
Photographs by Keven Peck Photography

SOUTHWIND CABERNET SAUVIGNON

GOURMET PAIRINGS
Pairs beautifully with a grilled coffee-rubbed ribeye steak.

TASTING NOTES
Concentrated black fruit aromas of boysenberry preserves, toasted bread, and wet gravel and earth created a rich, round mouthfeel that features soft, fine-grained tannins.

WINEMAKER'S INSIGHT
One hundred percent of the fruit comes from selected blocks at our estate Southwind Vineyard, then from barrel selections made in the winery. This wine is made in extremely small quantities.

AWARDS AND DISTINCTIONS
Gold Medal – Best of the Northwest: SIP Magazine
93 points – WineReviewOnline
91 points – Planet Grape
93 points – Blues Lifestyle

TECHNICAL DATA

APPELLATION: Walla Walla Valley
COMPOSITION: 90% Cabernet Sauvignon, 5% Malbec, 5% Petit Verdot
MATURATION: Aged in French oak barrels for 23 months; 60% first-fill barrels
CELLARING: Drinks beautifully now, and will continue to improve and open up with age for the next eight to 10 years

LEARN MORE

Visit our website by scanning image on left

Two of the Middleton family members play key roles in the day-to-day operations at Cadaretta Winery. Rick Middleton is the CEO and oversees all aspects of Cadaretta, and his sister, Kris Middleton, is involved with the event planning, tasting room, and social media and represents the family at most of the winery's events, reserve tastings, and dinners. Winemaker Peter Devison joined the team in 2017 after completing eighteen vintages of winemaking in both New Zealand and Washington State.

The full Cadaretta Winery experience includes a stop at the Tasting Gallery located in downtown Walla Walla. There, the story of the winery unfolds even more so, with old-growth wooden tables and walls decorated in large, oversized photos from the Middleton family's logging history.

TOP: Setting up for an in depth and educational Cadaretta Reserve Tasting of the estate wines. This Reserve Tasting is conducted by the Cadaretta Winemaker.

RIGHT: Cork souveniers at the Cadaretta Tasting Gallery, Downtown Walla Walla, Washington.
Photographs by Keven Peck Photography

Naturally, photos of the Cadaretta ship, loaded with timber, from the 1930s make a cameo, too. Even more special is the Glasshouse at the Southwind that sits atop the vineyard. Constructed out of sturdy red cedar timbers and rolling glass garage doors, it's a beautiful beacon on the land that likewise offers guests an incredible view of the entire Walla Walla Valley. Invite-only events and private tastings are hosted at Glasshouse throughout the year.

TOP: Picking Grapes during harvest at Southwind Vineyard.
Photograph by Kevin Peck Photography

RIGHT: Edward & Charles Middleton in front of a load of lumber waiting to be loaded onto the ship, *The Cadaretta*.
Photograph by Jones Photo Historical Collection

SOUTHWIND RED BLEND

GOURMET PAIRINGS

Pairs beautifully with a roasted rack of pork with a cherry bourbon sauce.

TASTING NOTES

This wine explodes with a nose of plum, black cherry, black currant, and spice including nutmeg and allspice. The mouthfeel exhibits a roundness with silky tannins, leading to a finish of oak, vanilla, cranberry, and pomegranate.

WINEMAKER'S INSIGHT

This blend of Bordeaux varietals come from selected blocks at our Southwind Vineyard, then from barrel selections made in the winery. This wine is made in very small quantities.

AWARDS & DISTINCTIONS

93 points – The Wine Advocate
90 points – Planet Grape
93 points – Blues Lifestyle

TECHNICAL DATA

APPELLATION: Walla Walla Valley
COMPOSITION: 37% Malbec, 37% Petit Verdot, 26% Cabernet Sauvignon
MATURATION: Aged in French oak barrels for 23 months; 60% first-fill barrels
CELLARING: Delicious now, and will continue to improve and evolve with age for the next six to eight years

ORDER OUR WINE

Visit our wine store by scanning the image to left

CANOE RIDGE VINEYARD WALLA WALLA

As legend has it, explorers Lewis and Clark noticed a ridge resembling an overturned canoe on their historic 1805 Columbia River journey. Today, that landmark is known as Canoe Ridge Vineyard, the namesake location of one of Washington State's most recognized wine producers. Established in the Horse Heaven Hills in 1989, followed by a Walla Walla-based winery in 1994, Canoe Ridge showcases wines to reflect the natural beauty and terroir of the Pacific Northwest.

At the helm of Canoe Ridge Vineyard is winemaker Bill Murray. Originally hailing from Napa, California, Bill has been making top-tier Bordeaux varieties and Chardonnay wines for more than 20 years. A close friend of longtime former Canoe Ridge Vineyard winemaker John Abbott, Bill took the helm in 2011 to focus on what the winery does best: Chardonnay, Merlot, and Cabernet Sauvignon. Today, Bill works primarily with French oak to subtly complement the structure of grapes from the Horse Heaven Hills.

For the wine drinker with a true Northwest taste for adventure, Canoe Ridge Vineyard reflects the natural beauty of the land and terroir. Whether sourced from our Horse Heaven Hills namesake vineyard or the surrounding Columbia Valley, Canoe Ridge Vineyard offers an authentic Northwest journey from one of Washington State's most recognizable wineries.

LEFT The exterior of the Canoe Ridge Winery, located in the historic Walla Walla Valley Railway Company Building.

ABOVE LEFT: A selection of Canoe Ridge Vineyard wines overlooking the sweeping landscape of the namesake vineyard, located in the Horse Heaven Hills.

ABOVE RIGHT: Winemaker Bill Murray inspects samples in the Canoe Ridge Vineyard Winery.
Photographs by Josiah Michael

COLLEGE CELLARS OF WALLA WALLA WALLA WALLA

Sometimes winemaking is more about the human investment than anything else, and College Cellars of Walla Walla proves that. The nonprofit teaching winery is making a big impact on Washington's wine industry, as well as internationally. Its goal is to go beyond research and train industry-ready viticulturalists and winemakers—and it's succeeding. Roughly 30 students per year graduate the program, and more than 175 have entered into the industry or started their own wineries. Students of all ages and backgrounds enter the two-year program and learn their craft on the eight-acre property located at the Center for Enology and Viticulture on the campus of Walla Walla Community College.

Founded in 2000 by Dr. Myles J. Anderson, College Cellars of Walla Walla is run by people who have a passion in viticulture. The advisory committee is comprised of some of Washington state's top winemakers and industry experts, including Elizabeth Bourcier, Chris Figgins, Rick Small, Dan Wampfler, and Victor Palencia. Their interest is always what is best for Washington wine, and it shows in the graduating student body. All proceeds from the winery go toward equipment, student needs, and scholarship funding.

College Cellars has events year-round, local release weekends, pouring events, and participates in festivals like Celebrate Walla Walla.

FACING PAGE: Grand Crew statue by artist Jeffrey Hill stands outside the Institute for Enology and Viticulture.
Photograph by Don Fleming

TOP : The staff of College Cellars of Walla Walla; Sabrina Lueck, Joel Perez, Marcus Rafanelli, Danielle Swan-Froese, Tim Donahue
Photograph by Steve Lenz

DOUBLEBACK WINERY WALLA WALLA

For former NFL quarterback Drew Bledsoe, his field of dreams always extended way beyond the stadium turf—all the way back to his Walla Walla Valley hometown and to the land of the grapes there. Even during his 14-year football career, which included time with the New England Patriots, Buffalo Bills, and Dallas Cowboys, he had his sights set on his post-game plan. Owning a winery was a longtime aspiration for the athlete, as it would allow him to combine his passion for fine wine with his love of the valley.

Upon his retirement in 2007, Drew returned home to plant his original estate vineyard, McQueen, on the southern end of the Walla Walla Valley AVA. The following year, in 2008, Drew launched Doubleback as an estate-focused winery with the goal to produce world-class Cabernet Sauvignon— the winery's name a reference to his return back home.

To make his dream a reality, Drew hired Winemaker and General Manager, Josh McDaniels. Josh, also a Walla Walla native, was named a "Game Changer of Washington Wine" by Wine Enthusiast and has most recently earned Doubleback's highest rating with 97 points from Robert Parker's Wine Advocate.

Since the very first release—the 2007 Cabernet Sauvignon—Doubleback has received numerous accolades including a spot on the Wine Spectator Top 100 List. The vision for Doubleback remains a premium wine experience completely focused on quality.

FACING PAGE: Biodiversity in full swing at Bob Healy Vineyard.

ABOVE: Drew & Maura Bledsoe enjoy a sunset bonfire at McQueen Vineyard.
Photographs by Andrea Johnson

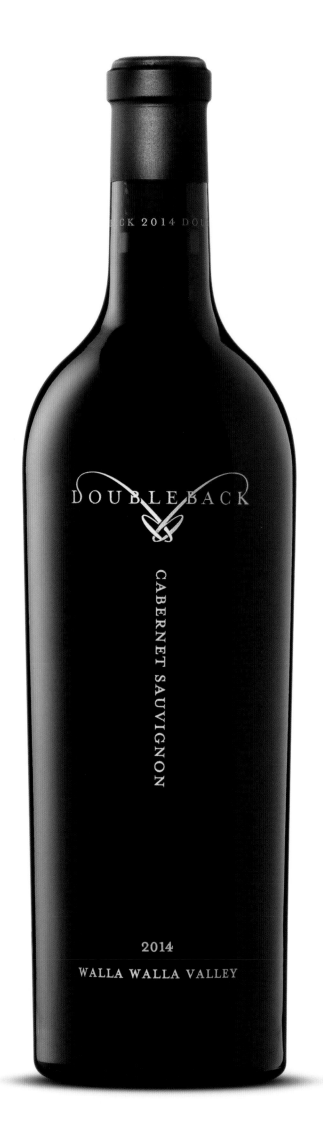

DOUBLEBACK CABERNET SAUVIGNON

GOURMET PAIRINGS

The savory nature of sous vide beef ribeye steak—featuring a quick pan sear—pairs well with the terroir while the fat of the steak balances out this structured wine.

TASTING NOTES

This Cabernet Sauvignon is made to be the perfect representation of the Walla Walla Valley and the distinct estate vineyards there. Doubleback walks a fine line to produce an elegant and structured cabernet that is approachable in its youth yet will age gracefully for decades.

WINEMAKER'S INSIGHT

Doubleback has a "vineyard first" winemaking approach. We meticulously manage our estate properties to have lots of airflow and sunlight while carrying light crop loads to ensure ripeness and balance. Our vineyard sites are spread out throughout the Walla Walla AVA so that we can naturally balance our wine to be a perfect representation of the Valley as a whole in a classic and elegant way—as beautifully demonstrated in our Cabernet Sauvignon.

AWARDS & DISTINCTIONS

97 points – Robert Parker's Wine Advocate
Top 100 List – Wine Spectator

TECHNICAL DATA

APPELLATION: Walla Walla Valley
COMPOSITION: 89% Cabernet Sauvignon, 8% Petit Verdot, 2% Malbec, 1% Merlot
MATURATION: Aged 22 months in French oak barrels and puncheons ranging from 65% new to 85% new.
CELLARING: May be enjoyed five years from vintage year or up to 15-20 years

VISIT OUR STORE

Order Doubleback wines in our store by scanning image on left.

To further assist the vision of high-quality, estate-focused wine, Drew has concentrated on developing individually distinct vineyard sites within the Walla Walla Valley AVA. In 2017, Doubleback also broke ground on a new winery facility slated for completion in early 2018.

For Drew and his wife, Maura, wine is not just about drinking enjoyment but also a compelling, layered experience. It is something to be shared and enjoyed; it's about romance, friendship, good conversation, and fellowship. They are committed to using only the most sustainable, superlative viticulture and winemaking practices to ensure that Doubleback is one of the best bottles around for that experience. All that to say, this football pro is clearly still making touchdowns—just on another kind of field.

TOP: Fall morning at McQueen Vineyard. Merlot block.
Photograph by Richard Duval

RIGHT: Doubleback Cabernet Sauvignon.
Photograph by Mark VanDonge

TOP: Bob Healy Vineyard in the Walla Walla Valley.
Photograph by Andrea Johnson

LEFT: Winemaker & GM Josh McDaniels and Proprietor Drew Bledsoe at the Doubleback Release Party.
Photograph by Mark VanDonge

STOLEN HORSE SYRAH

GOURMET PAIRINGS

Pairs wonderfully with pan-seared, fresh Northwest salmon and morel mushrooms.

TASTING NOTES

Stolen Horse Syrah is made in the same elegant style for which Doubleback Cabernet Sauvignon is known. With Syrah being such an ambassador of terroir, multiple "areas" of the Walla Walla Valley are blended together in order to create the best overall Syrah possible.

WINEMAKER'S INSIGHT

We purposefully select individual vineyard sites for the Syrah that are completely unique to each other. Once we pick the grapes, we do a mixture of whole cluster and destemmed fermentations in small lots with native and selected yeasts for long maceration times. We approach our Syrah almost like a Pinot Noir—it's a very hands-off process in the winery, trying to keep the wine as fresh as possible and truly let the vineyards and the Walla Walla Valley show through.

AWARDS & DISTINCTIONS

93 points – Wine Enthusiast

TECHNICAL DATA

APPELLATION: Walla Walla Valley
COMPOSITION: 95% Syrah, 5% Viognier (co-ferment)
MATURATION: Aged 18 months in French oak with about 25% new, puncheons and concrete tulips
CELLARING: May be enjoyed three years from vintage year or up to 10-15 years

LEARN MORE

Visit our website by scanning the image to left or visit www.doubleback.com

DUNHAM CELLARS WALLA WALLA

A keen palate and admiration for the art of crafting the perfect bottle of wine inspired founding winemaker, Eric Dunham, to start Dunham Cellars in 1995. Eric was drawn to wine from a young age. While in the Navy stationed at Moffett Field in Santa Clara County, he took as many trips as possible to Napa Valley. When asked by his father Mike what he wanted to do after the Navy, Eric had a clear vision: "I want to make wine." Not long after this declaration, Eric began his six-month internship at Hogue Cellars in Prosser, Washington. He was then hired as Assistant Winemaker at L'Ecole No. 41 in the Walla Walla Valley where, with Winemaker Marty Clubb's blessing, he began making small lots of Dunham wine. The first bottling was the 1995 Dunham Cabernet Sauvignon I. The first few vintages were released to great acclaim, and in 1999, Eric convinced his parents to help him launch Dunham Cellars in a World War II airplane hangar in Walla Walla.

Since then, Dunham Cellars has become one of the most celebrated wineries in the region. In 2004, the Dunham family invited David and Cheryll Blair to join them as winery co-owners, providing additional capital for future growth. Eric's passing in 2014, a year and a half after his father succumbed to his fight with kidney cancer, left the winery in the hands of his step-mother, Joanne Dunham, and the Blairs. Along with the rest of the Dunham Cellars winery family, Joanne and the Blairs continue Eric's vision of crafting consistently exceptional wines. The experience has also prompted the winery to give back to the community through various charitable events throughout the year.

FACING PAGE: Founding owner, Joanne Dunham spends her time event planning along with marketing for the winery. Accompanied by her faithful companions Maysy and Sadie.
Photograph by Cindy Anderson

ABOVE: Established in 1995, this family-owned winery in Walla Walla, produces ultra-premium wines with a tradition of excellence.
Photograph by Keven Peck

Two estate vineyards—Kenny Hill and Lewis—provide the foundation for Dunham Cellars wines. The Kenny Hill Estate Vineyard, named in honor of Winegrower Ken Hart, is located just a few miles east of the winery and spans 68 acres on a sloped, south-facing parcel of land. Fruit from this vineyard exhibits gorgeous concentration and vibrant acidity, thanks to cool temperatures from the nearby Blue Mountains. Here, Cabernet Sauvignon, Merlot, Syrah, Malbec, Petit Verdot, Grenache, and Chardonnay thrive.

The Lewis Estate Vineyard is nestled in the foothills of Rattlesnake Ridge in the Columbia Valley Appellation. The small family-owned vineyard managed by Betty Lewis and son Ken Jr., in close coordination with Ken Hart, includes 55 acres of grapes: Syrah, Cabernet Sauvignon, Merlot, Riesling, and Chardonnay. Dunham Cellars' inaugural 1999 Syrah was the first crop from Lewis Estate Vineyard, and it was simply remarkable.

ABOVE & BELOW: Kenny Hill Estate Vineyard is a south-facing sloped parcel at the foothills of the Blue Mountains. With elevation of 1,375-1,450 feet it was first planted in 2010.
Photograph by Keven Peck

TRUTINA BORDEAUX BLEND

GOURMET PAIRINGS

Pairs beautifully with our Spring Release Weekend tradition of hot fettuccine tossed in a Parmesan cheese wheel.

TASTING NOTES

Our premier red blend, Trutina offers aromas of ripe blackberry and dark chocolate that lead to complex layers of rich cocoa powder, brandied cherries and a hint of cola. Lush, well-integrated tannins weave seamlessly with the balanced acidity providing a lengthy finish. A sure-fire crowd pleaser!

WINEMAKER'S INSIGHT

Trutina means "balance" in Latin, and this is what we strive for each time we blend the noble Bordeaux varietals. When working with multiple lots, we have the opportunity to feature an array of varietal characters that offer a spectrum of different flavors, acidity, and tannin profiles. The art is finding a balance between tart fruit to sweet ripe fruit, and a lively amount of acid to accommodate the tannins. In the end, we want to leave you wanting more of this distinctive wine.

AWARDS & DISTINCTIONS

90+ points – Wine Enthusiast, Wine Spectator & Wine Advocate

TECHNICAL DATA

APPELLATION: Columbia Valley
COMPOSITION: Cabernet Sauvignon and Merlot dominant, with small percentages of Malbec, Cabernet Franc, and Petit Verdot
MATURATION: Aged 20 months in 60% new oak, a balance between French and American
CELLARING: Ready to drink now but can age eight-plus years

LEARN MORE

Learn more about this wine and our winery by scanning the image on the left

COLUMBIA VALLEY CABERNET SAUVIGNON

GOURMET PAIRINGS

During our Holiday Barrel Tasting Weekend, we serve our Columbia Valley Cabernet Sauvignon with Moroccan Lamb Stew over couscous. The spicy aromas of cinnamon, ginger, and allspice fill the nose and complement the wine perfectly.

TASTING NOTES

Opening aromas of dark fruit, pipe tobacco, and anise lead to a lively palate of ripe cherries, blackberry cobbler, and sage. Elegant tannins and bright acidity showcase a graceful, beautifully concentrated wine that pairs perfectly with food or shines on its own.

WINEMAKER'S INSIGHT

The cornerstone of Dunham Cellars winemaking is our Cabernet Sauvignon. Primarily estate fruit, we also seek some of the best outside vineyard sources throughout the Columbia Valley to help create this blend. This allows us to exhibit both dark and red fruit, as well as the savory elements of Cabernet Sauvignon. This wine always offers plenty of layers and complexity. It is approachable on release but is built with the structure to age.

AWARDS AND DISTINCTIONS

90+ rating – Wine Enthusiast, Wine Spectator & Wine Advocate

TECHNICAL DATA

APPELLATION: Columbia Valley
COMPOSITION: 100% Cabernet Sauvignon
MATURATION: Typically aged 20 months in French and American oak barrels; mostly new oak depending on vintage, usually around 70% French and 30% American
CELLARING: Ten-plus years is suggested

VISIT OUR STORE

Buy this wine by scanning image on left

With complete control over the winemaking process starting in the vineyards, Dunham Cellars ensures every bottle best expresses balance through its varietal character and terroir. That balance is apparent in every glass of Dunham Cellars wine when guests visit the winery in the Walla Walla Airport District. Maysy and Sadie, the two beloved winery dogs, escort visitors to the doors of the winery through a landscaped courtyard. Inside, two rooms await, offering two different experiences—the tasting bar and the Hangar Lounge. The tasting bar itself is a one-ton polished slab of Morton Gneiss, one of the oldest types of stone on Earth, and there is plenty of eclectic wine-centric merchandise available for purchase.

Through a large wooden door is the Hangar Lounge, where stunning artwork from Eric Dunham is showcased. The room is a renovated World War II-era hangar and is anchored by an enormous custom-made glass bottle tree. Occasionally during harvest, one of the original sliding doors is opened, to allow visitors to witness the crush pad where grapes begin their journey. Events include the Spring Kick-Off Weekend the first weekend of April, Spring Release Weekend the first weekend of May, Dunham Days! on the last weekend in August, Fall Release Weekend the first weekend of November, and the Holiday Barrel Tasting Weekend on the first weekend in December.

TOP: The Hangar Lounge is a renovated World War II-era hangar where wine tasting is enjoyed in its comfortable and eclectic décor.
Photograph by Andrea Johnson

ABOVE: The Dunham and Blair families share a passion for making their wine and winery a wonderful experience for all.
Photograph by Ashley Wondra

ETERNAL WINES WALLA WALLA

Wine isn't always about fancy names and designer labels, and Brad Binko, owner of Eternal Wines and its sister brand Drink Washington State, knows that. The latter takes all the pretense out of winemaking and offers drinkers approachable options that are suitable for every day of the week. But if you like big, age-worthy wines with fancy names and designer labels, he has that too.

Located in Walla Walla, Eternal Wines produces terroir-driven wines in small batches with a focus on single-vineyard Rhone varietals from hand-harvested fruit. Although the Syrah is worth trying, don't skip the whites. Grenache Blanc, Marsanne, Roussanne, and Viognier are much harder to find in the area and these varietals will not disappoint. Drink Washington State concentrates on blends and gets creative with grapes from appellations statewide. The results are ready-to-drink varietals that you'd welcome at your dinner table for any occasion.

Want to take a tour? Check out the winery's limo tours and travel through the vineyards in style. The winemaker serves as the tour guide and explains history, terroir, and flavor. Sip and sample at either of the tasting rooms: the cozy downtown location or the Airport Winery Tasting Room. Eternal Winery holds and participates in festivals and celebrations year-round, including Reveal Walla Walla, Guitarfest, and Taste Washington. For specific festival dates and times, call before planning your visit to either winery

FACING PAGE: Our Airport winery location where all the magic happens. Located at the Incubators. Winter is beautiful.
Photograph by Catherine Elizabeth Dobbins

TOP LEFT: We offer great variety of merchandise in both of our tasting rooms. Come accessorize yourself!
Photograph by Brad Binko

TOP RIGHT: Taking selfies with Picasso is always fun. Our motto is we only source from Picasso approved vineyards!
Photograph by Brad Binko

FIVE STAR CELLARS

For some, retirement might mean more tee times. But, for Five Star Cellars' David Huse, it watered the seed of a winemaking passion. He had always enjoyed wine, so when he began helping out at another Walla Walla Valley winery in 1999, it was only one short year before he decided to start his own.

His first vintage of 120 cases of Cabernet Sauvignon soon followed. In 2001, production increased, doubling the Cabernet and adding the same amount of Merlot. David began to realize that he needed a dedicated space to continue indulging his passion.

In August 2002, remodeling began at what now is the current site of Five Star Cellars. And, shortly thereafter in September, the first crush occurred at the winery, with the tasting room opening in December of that year.

As production continued to increase and Syrah was also added to the mix, David's son, Matt, began to take the reigns as winemaker, thus continuing the tradition of the family-fun business and allowing David to concentrate on marketing and distribution. The Five Star team has grown to now include Matt's wife, Traci, who manages the Wine Club and office operations. In 2010, Cameron Rushton joined as the Assistant Winemaker.

As for the name of the winery, well, it was selected to fulfill both David and Matt's ongoing dedication to producing "five star" quality red wines—including not only Syrah, Merlot, and Cabernet but also Malbec, Semillon, and Sangiovese—that are at the peak of excellence and class.

FACING PAGE: Traci Huse, Wine Club Manager; Matt Huse, Winemaker; Cameron Rushton, Assistant Winemaker.

TOP LEFT: Enjoy the mural by Jeff Hill on the front of the Five Star tasting room.

TOP RIGHT: Many of our wines at our tasting room can be purchased in different sized bottles.
Photographs by Dakotah Fryatt

FOUNDRY VINEYARDS WALLA WALLA

Mark and Patty Anderson have taken the art of winemaking to a whole new level at Foundry Vineyards. Indeed, the minute the modern white cube structure that serves as the tasting room comes into view, it's clear that this is no traditional wine experience. From the beginning, these founders-owners have integrated the discipline of modern and contemporary art into the wine experience, thus expanding the dialogue surrounding the creative processes that underlie the making of both wine and art.

Indeed, every element of Foundry has a distinct aesthetic—from the artistically inspired artisan labels, to the onsite gallery that features rotating exhibitions (past artists have included Chuck Close, Kiki Smith, and Ai Weiwei), to the minimalist, urban vibe of the outdoor sculpture garden.

The roots of Foundry Vineyards can be traced back to 1998, when Mark planted Cabernet Sauvignon and Merlot grapes on his residential property, which he named Stonemarker Vineyard. As a born and raised Walla Wallan, he saw his town evolving in the late '90s—in a good way—as wine was all the buzz and visitors were seeking out local wineries. Mark wanted to be a part of this new and exciting wine movement, and as a business entrepreneur with an artist's heart, he capitalized on the opportunity.

New to farming, Mark hired Scott Hendricks to help plant Stonemarker and initially sold the grapes to other Walla Walla wineries. But, in 2003, Mark decided to take everything he had learned about grapes and the winemaking

FACING PAGE: Lisa and Jay Anderson operate Foundry Vineyards as well as an independent design shop JOIN Shop Foundry.
Photograph by Krista Welch Creative

ABOVE: Foundry Vineyards tasting room offers guests the opportunity to taste their wines, view art in their contemporary gallery and sculpture garden, and shop in an independent design store.
Photograph courtesy of Foundry Vineyards

CABERNET SAUVIGNON

GOURMET PAIRINGS
Pairs well with dry-aged New York strip steak and mushroom risotto made with Walla Walla sweet onions and wild morel mushrooms.

TASTING NOTES
Our Cabernet Sauvignon is sourced entirely from the Walla Walla Valley and offers a bouquet of black cherries and currants with hints of thyme, rosemary, and saddle leather. The palate is full of rich dark chocolate, crème de cassis, and black currants.

WINEMAKER'S INSIGHT
This vintage was fermented in oak tanks then aged for 22 months in 70% new French oak before resting in the bottle for nine months prior to release. This wine can be consumed upon release or aged for many years.

AWARDS AND DISTINCTIONS
Foundry Vineyards frequently scores 90+ points in national wine publications.

TECHNICAL DATA

APPELLATION: Walla Walla Valley
COMPOSITION: 100% Cabernet Sauvignon
MATURATION: Aged 22 months in 70% new French oak barrels and 30% neutral French oak barrels
CELLARING: Delicious upon release, but can be cellared for up to 15 years

ORDER OUR WINES

Enter our store by scanning image on left or visit http://www.foundryvineyards.com

process and start a boutique winery. He held back fruit that year to create a small amount of his own wine to commemorate the work of his art clients at the Walla Walla Foundry—a company he and Patty established in 1980. The inaugural vintage was a blend of Cabernet and Merlot grapes that featured label artwork by renowned artist Jim Dine. This very wine would eventually serve as the basis for Foundry's flagship artisan blend.

Mark and Patty's affinity for art and wine was clearly passed down to their two children, Jay and Lisa, who now manage Foundry Vineyards. Jay is the creative director and winemaker, and Lisa is the sales and event manager. Most importantly, though, they continue to weave creativity throughout the winery. In 2017, they teamed up with JOIN Shop to create an intimate, design-centric gift shop for the winery's tasting room that features more than 50 independent designers with thoughtfully curated products ranging from handmade jewelry and ceramics, to leather goods, letterpress cards, and more.

Foundry Vineyards also hosts Hatha yoga sessions every Saturday in the art gallery—and occasionally the sculpture garden—adding another layer of peaceful, artistic expression to this one-of-a-kind winery experience.

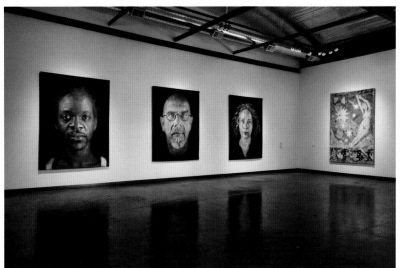

LEFT: Stonemarker Vineyard was planted in 1998 at the base of the Blue Mountains in Walla Walla.
Photograph courtesy of Foundry Vineyards

TOP: As brother and sister, Jay and Lisa, enjoy developing their family business of Art + Wine.
Photograph by Annelise Michelle Photography

MIDDLE: Foundry Vineyards hosts world-renowned artists in their gallery, artists such as Chuck Close and Kiki Smith.
Photograph courtesy of Foundry Vineyards

BOTTOM: Foundry Vineyards contemporary space is perfect for any artful celebration, including weddings!
Photograph by Luke and Mallory

HENRY EARL ESTATE WINES WALLA WALLA

Born from two families that know the lessons of hard work and what it takes to produce superior wines, comes Henry Earl Estate Wines. The name honors he owners' fathers, Henry Shaw and Earl West. The winery is dedicated to making wines that reflect the unique character and quality of our Red Mountain vineyards.

Henry Earl Estate Wines was only a dream back in 1981 when Dick Shaw planted 100 acres of vines near Mattawa. Together with his wife Wendy, the Shaws have now planted more than 3,000 acres in eastern Washington, more than 500 of which are located in the Red Mountain AVA. In 2014, Dick and Wendy brought their love of Washington wines to Walla Walla. Located in the historic Kennedy building in the heart of downtown, the Henry Earl Estates tasting room and wine bar embodies the energy of Walla Walla with a casual, laid back atmosphere. Guests are invited to come and sample wines, paired with a menu of small plates such as a fruit and cheese board, hummus and olives, and a selection of sweet treats.

The wines at Henry Earl focus on the Bordeaux varietals from Red Mountain. They produce a Sauvignon Blanc, Merlot, Malbec, Petit Verdot, Homesteader (a red blend), Cabernet Franc, and three Cabernet Sauvignons from each of the vineyards.

LEFT: Much in demand for its premium red grapes that produce bold, tannic wines, Quintessence Vineyards comprises the largest contiguous vineyard property on Red Mountain.

ABOVE RIGHT: Drawn exclusively from their major vineyards on Red Mountain, Dick and Wendy Shaw ensure that Henry Earl wines are crafted from premium grapes.

ABOVE LEFT: The Henry Earl team of Winemaker Mitch Venohr, General Manager Kasee Woods, and Vineyard Manager Marshall Edwards brings the best of Red Mountain grapes to its wines.
Photographs by Richard Duval

L'ECOLE N° 41   WALLA WALLA

A leap of faith—and a little old schoolhouse—are the forces that eventually propelled L'Ecole N° 41 managing winemaker and co-owners Marty Clubb and his wife, Megan, to move to the Walla Walla Valley permanently in 1989, leaving the business world in San Francisco behind in favor of the beautiful grape. They weren't too far from home though, so to speak, as the family-owned winery was originally founded by Megan's parents, Jean and Baker Ferguson, six years earlier—making it the third oldest winery in the valley.

As for what's in its name, for L'Ecole N° 41, the answer is just about everything. Translated from French, it means "the school," which is apropos given the winery was named for a historic 1915 schoolhouse in Frenchtown's Walla Walla school district number 41. That two-room schoolhouse now serves as the headquarters for the winery—and it's also the centerpiece art that's depicted on each wine label. The winery's restored Tasting Room occupies one of the two classrooms and preserves the schoolhouse character with original chalkboards, light fixtures, fir floors, and moldings. In the cellar, there's even a children's water fountain as well as a restored mural that was originally hand-painted by the school children for their Christmas pageant.

FACING PAGE: L'Ecole N° 41 located in the historic Frenchtown Schoolhouse built in 1915.

TOP RIGHT: Tasting L'Ecole N° 41's award-winning wines in the historic Frenchtown Schoolhouse is a must for wine lovers seeking the best from Washington State.
Photographs by Sander Olson

What's more, Frenchtown itself derived its name from the many French-Canadians who settled there during the early 1800s, eventually introducing the early roots of nurseries, vineyards, and winemaking to the region's growing economy. In this way, L'Ecole is not only an authentic, artisan winery built on experience and innovation, it also truly salutes its heritage and the pioneer viticulture efforts of the area.

ESTATE FERGUSON VINEYARD

GOURMET PAIRINGS

Perfect with pappardelle and veal ragout, or grilled organic filet mignon with gnocchi tossed in a creamy pesto sauce.

TASTING NOTES

Ferguson is L'Ecole N° 41's internationally acclaimed single vineyard Estate Bordeaux blend from Ferguson Vineyard—a stunning, high-elevation site overlooking the renowned Walla Walla Valley. The vines, planted on a ridge of fractured basalt from 15-million-year-old ancient lava flows, give this complex cabernet-dominant blend its bold dark fruit, immense structure, and dense minerality.

WINEMAKER'S INSIGHT

This site's unique individuality sets the stage for terroir-driven wines. Hand-selected from the oldest and most distinguished vineyard blocks, this collectible and age-worthy wine represents the best of L'Ecole.

AWARDS AND DISTINCTIONS

Best Bordeaux Blend in the World,
 Decanter World Wine Awards (2014), 2011 Ferguson
Best New World Bordeaux Blend,
 Six Nations Wine Challenge (2016), 2013 Ferguson

TECHNICAL DATA

APPELLATION: Walla Walla Valley
COMPOSITION: 56% Cabernet Sauvignon, 30% Merlot, 7% Cabernet Franc, 7% Malbec
MATURATION: Cleanly racked to 100% small French oak barrels, with several rackings over 22 months
CELLARING: May be enjoyed upon release or cellared up to 20 years

VISIT OUR STORE

Buy Ferguson or other L'Ecole wines at our store by scanning image on left

L'Ecole is engaged in growing and making 100 percent of their wines, where each bottle is handcrafted with a commitment to quality in the vineyards and the winery. With more than 35 years of winemaking experience, combined with dedicated, long-term relationships with some of the oldest and most proven vineyards in the Walla Walla and Columbia Valleys, L'Ecole has become one of the most trusted and respected brands in Washington State and has garnered national and international accolades over the years.

With that, L'Ecole N° 41 continues to pass the test of fine wine with flying colors.

TOP: Sustainable farming practices were fully implemented in preparing and planting Ferguson to qualify the vineyard as Certified Sustainable and Certified Salmon Safe.
Photograph by Andrea Johnson

RIGHT: A large, indigenous basalt rock quarried from the vineyard site serves as the foundation for the Ferguson Vineyard sign.
Photograph by Sander Olson

TOP: The Clubb family, (Left–Right) Marty, Megan, Rebecca and Riley, representing the 2nd and 3rd generation ownership of L'Ecole N° 41.

LEFT: Walla Walla Valley Vineyard Collection–three age-worthy, single vineyard Bordeaux blends which capture the individual nuances of each vineyard's unique terroir.
Photographs by Sander Olson

ESTATE MERLOT

GOURMET PAIRINGS

Pairs beautifully with pan-roasted quail accompanied by roasted beet hash and braised lentils.

TASTING NOTES

L'Ecole N° 41 is recognized as one of Washington State's leading producers of premium Merlot and this rich and generous estate vineyard blend represents one of the best. The elegance and old-world structure of Seven Hills Vineyard adds complexity to the earthiness and minerality of the basalt soil from Ferguson Vineyard. It's an impressively structured, cellar-worthy merlot that includes small quantities of cabernet franc and cabernet sauvignon.

WINEMAKER'S INSIGHT

L'Ecole N° 41's goal is to achieve stylistically expressive and aromatic wines that allow the vineyard's individual site characteristics to shine through. We believe in well-balanced wines, good acidity, firm but not over-powering tannins, complementary oak extraction, and vibrant, expressive aromas and fruit flavors—all fully celebrated in this blend.

AWARDS AND DISTINCTIONS

Consistently garners top scores and accolades from leading wine review publications.

TECHNICAL DATA

APPELLATION: Walla Walla Valley
COMPOSITION: 80% Merlot, 10% Cabernet Sauvignon, 10% Cabernet Franc, 50% Estate Ferguson Vineyard, 50% Estate Seven Hills Vineyard
MATURATION: Cleanly racked to 100% small French oak barrels, with several rackings over 18 months.
CELLARING: May be enjoyed upon release or cellared up to 15 years

ORDER OUR WINE

Buy our Estate Merlot or other L'Ecole wines at our store by scanning image on left

Long Shadows Vintners WALLA WALLA

Long Shadows Vintners is a collection of seven ultra-premium Columbia Valley wines showcasing the viticultural excellence of the growing region. Founded in 2003 by Washington State wine visionary Allen Shoup, the founding principle behind Long Shadows was as simple as it was complex: recruit a cadre of the finest winemakers in the world, give each vintner access to Washington State's best grapes, and outfit a winery to accommodate a diverse group of winemakers' cellar specifications. The idea quickly sold itself, and from the beginning, Long Shadows' unique portfolio has been embraced by critics and consumers alike.

The project is a continuation of Shoup's life-long ambition to highlight the world-class quality of Washington wines. Widely recognized as one of the founding fathers of the Washington wine industry, Shoup led Chateau Ste. Michelle and its affiliates for two decades. An entrepreneur at heart, he left the consortium in 2000 to begin working on his own project named for the "long shadows" cast by the iconic international winemakers Shoup brought to the state. Each winemaker uses Washington grapes to design a single wine reflective of the style for which he is best known. Central to the success of Long Shadows is Gilles Nicault, director of winemaking and viticulture. Based in Walla Walla, Nicault has led Long Shadows winemaking from the start. It is his job to oversee the daily operations of the winery and make sure each winemaker's vision and style is honored in the vineyard and the cellar.

The French-born Nicault describes his work as the "dream job." His zest for life and continual curiosity fuel the creation of Long Shadows' diverse offerings.

FACING PAGE: Washington wine visionary and Long Shadows founder Allen Shoup brought celebrated vintners from around the globe to the Columbia Valley to showcase the viticultural excellence of the growing region.
Photograph by Joann Arruda - THE TASTING PANEL

ABOVE: Long Shadows' state-of-the-art winery is located in the rolling hills of the Walla Walla Valley.
Photograph by Jack von Eberstein

CHESTER-KIDDER RED WINE

GOURMET PAIRINGS
Pair with braised short ribs and roasted root vegetables.

TASTING NOTES
Expressive aromas and flavors of ripe black cherries, oak spice, violets, and a hint of graphite offer this wine depth and complexity. Its rich texture and firm yet refined tannins linger across a lengthy finish that showcase the limited-production wine's vibrant character. Extended macerations of 40 days give the wine supple tannins that stand up to 30 months of barrel aging in tight-grained 85 percent new French oak barrels. Integrated fruit that enhances the mid-palate, an extra layer of complexity, and an earthy finish make it a favorite.

WINEMAKER'S INSIGHT
More than half the grapes used in the Chester-Kidder Red Wine were grown on Red Mountain and surrounding vineyards, which give the wine its firm structure and pleasant intensity. Walla Walla Valley vineyards comprise another significant portion of the blend, contributing dark, rich textures to the wine. Grapes from Weinbau Vineyard on the Wahluke Slope add a layer of ripe, fresh flavors and refined tannins.

AWARDS & DISTINCTIONS
Red Blend of the Year – Washington Wine Awards
Served to French President Francois Hollande at White House State Dinner, February 2014

TECHNICAL DATA

APPELLATION: Columbia Valley
COMPOSITION: Primarily Cabernet Sauvignon, with Syrah and Petit Verdot
MATURATION: Aged 30 months in 100% French oak, 85% new
CELLARING: Enjoy now with gentle decanting, and will cellar well for at least 12 years

LEARN MORE

Learn more about Chester Kidder by scanning image on left or visiting www.longshadows.com

He graduated from the University of Avignon with a degree in Viticulture and Enology and honed his craft in the vineyards and wineries of Côtes du Rhône, Provence, and Champagne. In 1994, Nicault moved to Washington for an internship and was so taken by the growing region he decided to stay. Nicault joined Woodward Canyon in 1996, where he was named head of enology and production before moving to Long Shadows in 2003. Under Nicault's careful and adventurous eye, Long Shadows produces a select offering of red and white wines that capture the spirit of the winemaker while allowing the fruit to express itself. He was named Winemaker of the Year at the 2016 Washington Wine Awards.

Food & Wine magazine named Long Shadows its "Winery of the Year" in 2007, just four years after its founding. A description of Long Shadows wines, all remarkably rated 90+ every year since each wine's debut vintage, follows.

Randy Dunn, known for his work with Cabernet Sauvignon at Napa Valley's Caymus Vineyards as well as his own label, Dunn Vineyards, crafts Feather. With its impressive balance of intensity and elegance, Feather is a firmly-structured wine that showcases the best of what Columbia Valley Cabernet Sauvignon has to offer.

Michel Rolland lends his talents to the Pedestal Merlot, an acclaimed wine that earned a spot on Wine Spectator's Top

TOP: Long Shadows dream team of international vintners travel to Washington regularly to visit the vineyards and assemble final blends. Left to Right: Gilles Nicault, Michel Rolland, Allen Shoup, John Duval, Philippe Melka, Randy Dunn. *Photograph courtesy of Long Shadows Vintners*

BELOW: Guest amenities at the Walla Walla winery include an expansive patio, outdoor fire pit and two pétanque courts. *Photograph by Jack von Eberstein*

100 Wines, among other honors. Based in Pomerol, Rolland consults for over 100 vintners around the world. Highly acclaimed by critics, his Washington Merlot is a deeply-concentrated wine with intense aromas, luxurious flavors, and a bold finish.

Pirouette, an enticing Bordeaux-style red blend named to Wine Enthusiast's Top 100 Cellar Selections list, is the work of Napa Valley's Philippe Melka. It was through a winemaking assignment with Napa Valley's Quintessa and resulting friendship with Quintessa owner Agustin Huneeus Sr., that Philippe was introduced to Shoup and Long Shadows. Melka spent time at Château Haut-Brion and Petrus, and his winemaking talents are well-known. Influential wine critic Robert Parker named him one of the top nine winemakers in the world, and Melka's expertise is apparent in Pirouette.

Long Shadows' Saggi is another of the winery's notable offerings. Inspired by Ambrogio and Giovanni Folonari, a father-son team from one of Tuscany's most prestigious wine families, Saggi is

TOP LEFT: Sunrise on Syrah grapes shortly before harvest. Exposed clusters shown on the right side allow the morning sun to fully reach each cluster. The protected fruit zone on the left side shields grapes from the harsh afternoon sun.
Photograph by Richard Duval Images

BELOW LEFT: The Benches is an extraordinary vineyard of beauty and scope, carved out of a steep cliff on the edge of the Columbia River.
Photograph by Kathryn Elsesser

ABOVE: The fermentation process for each red wine varies, according to each winemaker's exacting specifications.
Photograph by Kathryn Elsesser

FEATHER CABERNET SAUVIGNON

GOURMET PAIRINGS
Pairs perfectly with Boeuf Bourguignon.

TASTING NOTES

A sophisticated wine with an impressive balance of intensity and elegance, the Feather Cabernet Sauvignon offers generous aromas of black cherries and dried rosemary, as well as nuances of French oak. The firmly-structured wine features a soft and rich palate as the wine's dark fruit flavors glide over refined tannins for a long, pleasurable finish.

WINEMAKER'S INSIGHT

Hand-harvested grapes were sorted, lightly crushed, and fermented in stainless steel tanks and received aggressive pump-overs two to three times a day to extract structure and color. As fermentation neared completion, pump-overs became gentler to coax out delicate tannins and texture.

AWARDS & DISTINCTIONS

Rated 90-plus points each year since its debut vintage

TECHNICAL DATA

APPELLATION: Columbia Valley
COMPOSITION: Cabernet Sauvignon
MATURATION: Aged 22 months in 90% new Vicard French oak barrels
CELLARING: Enjoy now with gentle decanting, yet will cellar well for at least 15 years

LEARN MORE

Learn more about Feather by scanning image on left or visiting www.longshadows.com

a soft, silky wine that packs a flavorful punch, loaded with wild berries, fresh plums, and hints of oak spice. Nicault now oversees the winemaking responsibilities for Saggi.

Australia's John Duval crafts Sequel Syrah. Duval began his career in winemaking with Penfolds in 1974, and in his nearly three-decade tenure there, including 16 years as chief winemaker, accumulated numerous international awards most famously as the winemaker for Penfolds Grange. He left Penfolds in 2002 to establish John Duval Wines and shortly thereafter joined Long Shadows. His winemaking hand is evident in Sequel's rich, concentrated style.

Chester-Kidder Red Wine, named in honor of Shoup's mother Elizabeth Chester, and grandmother Maggie Kidder, is Nicault's creation. A New World blend of Cabernet Sauvignon, Syrah, and other Bordeaux varieties, Chester-Kidder is prized by collectors for its complexity, elegance, and refined tannins. It is one of three Long Shadows wines to be served at a White House state dinner.

Nicault also crafts Poet's Leap Riesling, Long Shadows' sole white wine offering. The wine was originally inspired by Armin Diel, owner of Schlossgut Diel in Germany, one of the most respected producers of Riesling in the world. One of America's most acclaimed Rieslings, Poet's Leap has twice been named to Wine Enthusiast's Top 100 Wines list.

Long Shadows carefully sources grapes from Washington's best vineyards. From The Benches, a sustainably-farmed vineyard in Horse Heaven Hills and Sagemoor in the Columbia Valley

FACING PAGE: Long Shadows sources grapes from the best vineyards in the state, including the Benches in the Horse Heaven Hills AVA..
Photograph courtesy of Long Shadows Vintners

ABOVE: Gilles Nicault has led Long Shadows winemaking since the winery's founding. He was named Washington Winemaker of the Year in 2016.
Photograph by Richard Duval Images

established in 1972, to Boushey in Yakima Valley, StoneTree on the Wahluke Slope, Red Mountain vineyards, and Conner Lee and Candy Mountain in the Columbia Valley, Long Shadows showcases a wealth of fruit diversity from across the state. It's easy to see how Long Shadows has established a legacy of award-winning wines for itself and has become a benchmark for excellence.

With its emphasis on quality and its team of talented winemakers, the wines sells out quickly each year. However, guests can make reservations at either of the winery's two tasting room to sample the portfolio. In Walla Walla, guests enjoy a leisurely seated tasting while viewing the work of acclaimed glass artist and Washington native Dale Chihuly. A visit to the Woodinville tasting room, just 30 minutes northeast of Seattle, also provides guests with a relaxing visit, reiterating Long Shadows' diversity in offerings and experiences.

TOP: In addition to bringing an international team of celebrated vintners to Washington, founder Allen Shoup recruited his family (shown here) to execute on his vision for Long Shadows. Left-Right: Dane Narbaitz, Sara Narbaitz, Allen Shoup, Kathleen Shoup, Ryan Shoup

RIGHT: Industry veterans Dane Narbaitz (president), Allen Shoup (founder) and Gilles Nicault (director, winemaking and viticulture) have committed Long Shadows to quality every step of the way.
Photographs by Colby Kuschatka

PEDESTAL MERLOT

GOURMET PAIRINGS
Pair with seared venison medallions, morel mushroom risotto, and butternut squash.

TASTING NOTES
A deeply concentrated wine, the Pedestal Merlot features wonderfully intense aromas of dark cherry, violet, and marionberry. Ripe blackberry flavors framed by notes of oak spice, roasted coffee beans, and bittersweet chocolate provide the wine with a bold finish.

WINEMAKER'S INSIGHT
The hand-harvested fruit was double-sorted before fermentation to ensure stems and jacks were removed to avoid harsh tannins. The majority of the lots were cold-soaked to build richness and flavor before the fruit underwent whole-berry fermentation in 1,500-gallon upright French wood tanks. Gentle pump-overs throughout fermentation added to the enhanced color and richness on the palate.

AWARDS & DISTINCTIONS
Merlot of the Year – Washington Wine Awards
Washington Wine of the Year – The Seattle Times Wine Awards
Served at the White House holiday dinner
Served to French President Nicolas Sarkozy at the White House

TECHNICAL DATA

APPELLATION: Columbia Valley
COMPOSITION: Predominantly Merlot, with some Cabernet Sauvignon, Malbec, and Petit Verdot
MATURATION: Aged 22 months in 100% French oak, 85% new
CELLARING: Can be enjoyed now, and will cellar well for at least 10 years

LEARN MORE

Learn more about Pedestal by scanning image on left or visiting www.longshadows.com

PEDESTAL

COLUMBIA VALLEY
MERLOT
2025

FROM THE LONG SHADOWS
VINTNERS COLLECTION

PIROUETTE RED WINE

GOURMET PAIRINGS

Enjoy with smoked beef tenderloin, Yukon gold potato crisp and shaved horseradish.

TASTING NOTES

The Pirouette Red Wine is multi-layered with aromas and flavors of dark fruits and hints of sweet oak, licorice, and cocoa. Flavors gain complexity across the palate, while richly-textured, refined tannins and a luscious mouthfeel provide a delightful finish.

WINEMAKER'S INSIGHT

A variety of fermentation processes contribute to the complexity of this wine. Hand-harvested Cabernet berries were fermented in 400-liter French oak barrels that were gently rolled during fermentation. The technique gives the wine a fully-integrated oak flavor. All other varieties in the wine were fermented in traditional stainless steel tanks. Select lots enjoyed longer skin contact to enhance the wine's dark color and mid-palate.

AWARDS & DISTINCTIONS

Top 100 Cellar Selections (#2) Wine Enthusiast, 98 points

TECHNICAL DATA

APPELLATION: Columbia Valley

COMPOSITION: A Bordeaux blend of Cabernet Sauvignon, Petit Verdot, Merlot, and Cabernet Franc

MATURATION: Aged 22 months in 100% French oak, 75% new, before bottling, unfiltered and unfined

CELLARING: Enjoy now or cellar for 10 years or more

LEARN MORE

Learn more about Pirouette by scanning image on left or visiting www.longshadows.com

PIROUETTE

2015

FROM THE LONG SHADOWS
VINTNERS COLLECTION

TOP: The Walla Walla tasting room showcases a stunning glass art collection featuring the work of world-renowned artist Dale Chihuly.
Photograph courtesy of Long Shadows Vintners

RIGHT: Long Shadows' Woodinville tasting room offers a comfortable, relaxed setting for sampling the winery's collection of award-winning wines.
Photograph by Stephanie Cristalli

SAGGI RED WINE

GOURMET PAIRINGS
Pair with wild king salmon, whipped potatoes, and tarragon-mustard beurre blanc.

TASTING NOTES
Red currant and cassis aromas wrap around a core of licorice in this intensely colored wine. It's soft and silky on the entry with a flavorful package loaded with wild berries, fresh plums, and hints of oak spice complemented by a lively acidity and firmly textured mid-palate with a silky finish.

WINEMAKER'S INSIGHT
Small lots of hand-harvested grapes were brought to the winery and crushed using a technique known as saignée in which five to 10 percent of the grapes' juice is removed from the tank to enhance concentration. Extended maceration for an average of 30 days in small two-ton tanks provided optimal extraction to broaden the finished wine's mid-palate.

AWARDS & DISTINCTIONS
Rated 90-plus points each year since its debut vintage

TECHNICAL DATA

APPELLATION: Columbia Valley
COMPOSITION: A Super Tuscan-styled blend of Sangiovese, Cabernet Sauvignon, and Syrah
MATURATION: Aged 18 months in 100% French oak, 55% new
CELLARING: Enjoy this wine anytime in the next eight years

LEARN MORE

Learn more about Saggi by scanning image on left or visiting www.longshadows.com

SEQUEL SYRAH

GOURMET PAIRINGS

Enjoy with rack of lamb, balsamic-shallot crust, demi-glaze and potato gratin.

TASTING NOTES

A range of spices including nutmeg and cardamom are featured in this intensely colored and flavored wine. Sequel is rich in texture and packed with vibrant blackberry and cherry flavors. Delicious hints of roasted meats and black olive tapenade tickle the palate. The wine finishes with a vibrant, lively finish.

WINEMAKER'S INSIGHT

Portions of the grapes were fermented via an Australian method known as "rack and return." This technique requires the winemaker to drain the tank twice daily and gently pour the juice back in over the top of the skins. This gentle method helps extract richness from the Syrah's delicate berries without imparting bitter tannins. Whole-cluster fermentation enhanced richness and dimension on the palate. Some lots underwent submerged cap fermentation to add structure and enhance mouthfeel.

AWARDS & DISTINCTIONS

Rated 90-plus points each year since its debut vintage

TECHNICAL DATA

APPELLATION: Columbia Valley
COMPOSITION: Predominantly Syrah, with a small amount of Cabernet Sauvignon
MATURATION: Aged 18 months in 100% French oak barrels, 65% new
CELLARING: Can be enjoyed now, or cellar for up to 10 years or more

LEARN MORE

Learn more about Sequel by scanning image on left or visiting www.longshadows.com

Pepper Bridge Winery WALLA WALLA

Named for the old military road running from Fort Walla Walla to Fort Dalles, which forded the river at the Pepper family farm, Pepper Bridge Winery pays homage to Washington's pioneering spirit in everything it does. Owned and operated by three families—the McKibbens, the Goffs, and the Pellets—the winery produces Bordeaux-style wines from mature estate vineyards while integrating modern innovation into the process.

Norm McKibben began planting grapes in 1989 and throughout the Walla Walla Valley in the 1990s. He founded Pepper Bridge Winery in partnership with Anheuser-Busch veteran Ray Goff in 1998, and the next year, they brought third-generation Swiss winemaker, Jean-François Pellet, on as the final expert in the trio, who received distinction as 2015 Winemaker of the Year from the Washington Wine Awards. First and foremost, McKibben, Goff, and Pellet view themselves as stewards of the land. Every decision—from planting to integrating new technology into the winery—is done with an eye toward the goal of making quality wine while leaving the soil healthier for the next generation. As managing partner of the winery, Norm McKibben brings his vision and expertise as a trained engineer to the growth of Pepper Bridge Winery and the larger Walla Walla Valley AVA. His son, Eric McKibben, is actively involved as a partner.

With 30 years at Anheuser-Busch where he served as vice president of corporate purchasing and president of the company's agriculture subsidiary,

LEFT: Jean-François Pellet and Norm McKibben in the Pepper Bridge Winery barrel room.
Photograph by Amy Allen Photography

TOP: Evenings are magical at the Pepper Bridge tasting room overlooking the Pepper Bridge Vineyard in Walla Walla.
Photograph by Jack von Eberstein

PEPPER BRIDGE TRINE

GOURMET PAIRINGS

Pairs extremely well with a variety of dishes including roast leg of lamb, hearty pasta, and filet.

TASTING NOTES

Cabernet Franc often takes the lead in Trine, showing red berries, which highlight its energy and bright acidity. Notes of ripe raspberry, orange oil, and violet mingle toward a finish reminiscent of herbs de Provence. The palate of lush red fruit and raspberry compote gives the wine a fresh and flirtatious flavor.

WINEMAKER'S INSIGHT

The name, "Trine" rhymes with wine and is defined as a close group of three. The wine pays homage to the three families of Pepper Bridge—the McKibbens, Goffs, and Pellets—and hails from estate vineyards in the Walla Walla Valley. The fruit expresses itself more freely than other Pepper Bridge offerings, each year presenting consumers with a unique combination of the five traditional Bordeaux red grapes.

AWARDS & DISTINCTIONS

Consistent 90-plus scores across the industry
Top 100 Winery Worldwide seven times – Wine & Spirits

TECHNICAL DATA

APPELLATION: Walla Walla Valley
COMPOSITION: Cabernet Franc, Cabernet Sauvignon, Merlot, Malbec, Petit Verdot
MATURATION: Aged approximately 17 months in 100% French oak barrels
CELLARING: Delicious upon release and maintains vibrancy for years to come

VISIT OUR WEBSITE STORE

Enter our store by scanning image on left or visit
www.http://pepperbridge.orderport.net/wines/

Ray Goff developed a love of wine, leading him to co-found Pepper Bridge Winery. His daughter and business partner, Travis Goff, is also a partner of the winery. The winery was the first gravity flow winery in the state—complete with subterranean caves—and winemaker Jean-François Pellet helped develop and design a new optical sorter that improved the overall quality of the wine. In fact, Pellet's dedication to sustainable wine extends to his role as a founding member of VINEA, Walla Walla Valley's sustainable viticulture program.

As the winery moves into the next generation, the founders and partners continue to help cultivate the Washington industry and facilitate environmentally-conscious processes through its Old-World philosophy and modern innovation. With a portfolio of elegant, balanced wines that focus on Cabernet Sauvignon, Merlot, and the winery's Bordeaux blend, Trine, Pepper Bridge Winery has been named to Wine & Spirits' Top 100 Wineries list multiple years. The terroir-driven wines are crafted using traditional winemaking techniques, 100 percent French oak barrels, and 100 percent estate fruit from the Walla Walla Valley. Guests can explore the winery and sample its award-winning offerings via a private winery tour or exclusive food and wine pairing events.

TOP: Stainless steel fermentation tanks in the gravity-flow production facility.
Photograph by Jack von Eberstein

BOTTOM: The Walla Walla Valley Blue Mountains overlooking the Seven Hills Vineyard.
Photograph by Rose Pingree

Reynvaan Family Vineyards WALLA WALLA

Started in 2005 by husband-and-wife team Mike and Gale Reynvaan and their three adult children, Amanda, Angela, and Matt, Reynvaan Family Vineyards is a small, family-owned and operated winery with two estate vineyards located in the Walla Walla Valley. Their first vineyard in Milton-Freewater, Oregon, is one of the most unique terroirs in the country, aptly named "In the Rocks." The stunning location is a dried-up riverbed with soils that have resulted from an alluvial fan formed by the Walla Walla River some 15,000 years ago. Covered with large, smooth river rocks, the vineyard was first planted in 2005, and produces high-end Rhône-style red and white grapes, primarily Syrah, Viognier, Marsanne, and Grenache Blanc. Since the first vintage in 2007, these wines have been well received and highly acclaimed, both domestically and internationally. The vineyard also now produces Cabernet Sauvignon, Merlot, Cabernet Franc, and Petit Verdot.

In 2008, the family planted a second vineyard outside of Walla Walla in the Blue Mountains, called "Foothills in the Sun" at elevations of 1,500 to 1,600 feet; the vineyard flourished with Syrah, Viognier, and a little bit of Cabernet Sauvignon. The site is one of the highest elevation vineyards in Washington and is situated with a gradual western and southwesftern exposure. Temperatures can vary dramatically, from the 90s to a chilly 40 degrees at night, which helps to retain natural acidity and freshness in the wines. The soils here consist of deep silty loam with small amounts to clay, iron, and pockets of rocks.

FACING PAGE: Looking East towards the Blue Mountains at the "Foothills in the Sun" Vineyard.

TOP LEFT: Matt Reynvaan laying out the new "Foothills in the Sun" Vineyard.
Photographs by Gale Reynvaan

"STONESSENCE" SYRAH

GOURMET PAIRINGS

Canlis Seattle Restaurant's A5 Miyazaki ribeye, with spring onions, mushrooms, and sansho peppers.

TASTING NOTES

This 100% Syrah explodes with butcher shop-like aromas, salty cured meats, dense campfire smoke, and black olives, along with black fruits and ponzu sauce. This wine offers a seamless integration of oak, fine-grain tannin, and a deep richness.

WINEMAKER'S INSIGHT

Winemaker and vineyard manager Matt Reynvaan, ensures that vines are farmed organically, with no herbicides or pesticides. Using only native yeasts from their grapes each year, he lets the fruit ferment in open tanks, then ages it exclusively in French oak barrels for 18 to 24 months. The consistent result has been elegant, intense, and expressive wines that represent each of their distinct terroirs.

AWARDS AND DISTINCTIONS

Rated 98 points – Wine Spectator Magazine
#11 in the world – Wine Spectator Magazine.

TECHNICAL DATA

APPELLATION: Walla Walla Valley
COMPOSITION: 100% Syrah
MATURATION: Aged 18 to 24 months in oak barrels
CELLARING: May be cellared for 20 years or longer

LEARN MORE

Visit our website by scanning image on left

The winery is a family affair, Matt is the winemaker and vineyard manager who ensures that the wines remain dynamic, possess a depth of flavor, and offer a consistent finish. Nearly everything they do is by hand, including planting the vines, trellising, pruning, dropping fruit, and picking and sorting the berries at harvest. Amanda and Angela share responsibilities for customer relations, compliance, and other business operations. It's a labor of love for the entire team—and the entire team is all in. As an estate winery, only Reynvaan Family Vineyard grapes are used to produce the wines.

Over the last ten years, the vineyards have produced more than 40 wines with international critics' scores of 95 and higher, but two wines stand out. The 2010 "Stonessence" is a 100 percent Syrah from the In the Rocks vineyard selected by Wine Spectator as the number 11 wine in the world.

TOP: The winery building during winter in Walla Walla.

RIGHT: Spring pruning in the :Foothills in the Sun" Vineyard.
Photographs by Gale Reynvaan

It was rated at 98 points—the magazine's highest score ever for a Washington red wine—while Wine Advocate awarded it 96 points. Similarly, the 2013 In the Rocks Syrah co-fermented with Viognier, was ranked at as the number 13 wine in the world and rated at 97 points.

The family very much appreciates critical recognition but it's not why they produce their signature style of wine. They simply take what the vineyards give them each year and try to protect the purity, complexity, and natural flavors of the grapes. The goal has always been to produce some of the best Rhône-style varietals in the world from their two vineyards in Walla Walla Valley. They love their wines and hope others do as well.

TOP: Looking south towards the Seven Hills Vineyard from the "In the Rocks" Vineyard.

RIGHT: A detail showing the spring prining in the "In the Rocks" Vineyard.
Photographs by Gale Reynvaan

"IN THE ROCKS" SYRAH

GOURMET PAIRINGS

Chef Wolfgang Puck's rack of lamb with eggplant puree and harissa aioli.

TASTING NOTES

Incredibly dark and almost opaque in appearance, this Syrah/Viognier co-ferment has a floral bouquet of peach, apricot, and black tea that gives way to Asian five-spice, soy sauce, mushrooms, and slowly braised wagyu beef. It's extremely rich and concentrated.

WINEMAKER'S INSIGHT

Winemaker and vineyard manager Matt Reynvaan, ensures that vines are farmed organically, with no herbicides or pesticides. Using only native yeasts from their grapes each year, he lets the fruit ferment in open tanks, then ages it exclusively in French oak barrels for 18 to 24 months. The consistent result has been elegant, intense, and expressive wines that represent each of the distinct terroirs.

AWARDS & DISTINCTIONS

97 points – Wine Spectator Magazine.
#13 in the world – Wine Spectator Magazine

TECHNICAL DATA

APPELLATION: Walla Walla Valley
COMPOSITION: 95% Syrah, co-fermented with 5% Viognier
MATURATION: Aged 18 to 24 months in oak barrels.
CELLARING: May be cellared for 20 years or longer

LEARN MORE

Visit our website by scanning image on left

SLEIGHT OF HAND CELLARS WALLA WALLA

One would be hard-pressed to find a winery that didn't take winemaking seriously, but at Sleight of Hand Cellars, serious wine without serious attitudes is more than a slogan; it's a way of life. With wine names like The Enchantress, The Spellbinder, and Psychedelic Syrah, and with turntables and LP's in each tasting room, the winery is full of fun and a few surprises. Founded in 2007 by Trey Busch and Jerry and Sandy Solomon, Sleight of Hand Cellars stands out in the industry with its world-class wines, iconic label art, and "cut-loose," over-the-top tasting room experience. Named one of "The Next Generation" wineries of Washington State and one of "The Next Cult Wineries" by Seattle Magazine, along with being rated as having the most-fun tasting room in Washington State by multiple publications, Sleight of Hand is a winery for the modern age.

Using a combination of estate and non-estate vineyards from some of the best sites in the state, the winemaking team of Jerry Solomon, Trey Busch, and Keith Johnson crafts wines that get better every year, causing industry experts like the Wine Advocate to gush: "While I've always loved the wines from these guys, they've hit a new level recently, and the wines are now up there with the crème de la crème of the state (and beyond)."

Since the winery's founding, Busch and the Solomons have seen their dream grow from a small rented storefront location to a full-blown tasting room and production facility, and then the expansion to a tasting room in the SODO

FACING PAGE: Ziggy Stardust Syrah Block at Elevation Vineyard, located in the foothills of the Blue Mountains in the far, SE corner of the Walla Walla Valley.
Photograph by Trey Busch

ABOVE: Our winemaking team at Sleight of Hand, Keith Johnson, Jerry Solomon, and Trey Busch.
Photograph by Amy Allen

area of Seattle. When you step foot in either tasting room, you immediately realize that Sleight of Hand Cellars is no ordinary winery. With over 2,000 albums from various musical genres and turntables spinning vinyl in both tasting rooms—and the Wine Club Lounge at the Walla Walla property—Sleight of Hand excels at providing a unique experience in as many ways as possible. Music inspires each Sleight of Hand wine—music is always playing in the production facility—and the winemaking team feels there is magic in every bottle they produce. The Wine Illusionist Society, Sleight of Hand's exclusive wine club, enjoys the winery's collaboration with Sub Pop Records in Seattle. Every shipment of wine also includes a free digital download of some of the best songs from Sub Pop's current musicians.

Each wine features a magically inspired name and a label inspired by vintage magic posters. From the Levitation Syrah, a 92-point wine described as having an underlying funkiness of blackberry, blueberry compote, pepper, and wild herb-styled

aromas and flavors, to The Archimage Cab Franc/Merlot Blend with its enchanting aromas of Asian spices, red fruits, licorice, and dried herbs, Sleight of Hand Cellars has something for every taste.

TOP LEFT: Winter snow blanketing the slopes of our Ziggy Stardust Block at Elevation Vineyard.
Photograph by Trey Busch

BELOW LEFT: The rocky soils of Stoney Vine Vineyard produce some of the most distinctive Syrahs in the world.
Photograph by Amy Allen

ABOVE: Owners Sandy and Jerry Solomon, foot crushing our Estate Syrah from Stoney Vine Vineyard in the Walla Walla Valley.
Photograph by Trey Busch

THE ILLUSIONIST CABERNET SAUVIGNON

GOURMET PAIRINGS

Pair the Illusionist with a nice, well-marbled, prime or wagyu ribeye steak, potato skins crammed full of bacon, cheddar cheese, and sour cream, and a generous helping of great music; we recommend some mid-60s Rolling Stones, say, maybe "Aftermath," followed by Side One of Pearl Jam's Vitalogy.

TASTING NOTES

The Illusionist is dark, savory, and full-bodied, while remaining balanced and elegant. It is compelling, filled with aromas of cedar, tobacco, graphite, and a hint of fennel and vanilla. Dark notes of blackberry and cassis explode on entry, quickly followed by dark cherry and savory herbal flavors that linger for an extended finish.

WINEMAKER'S INSIGHT

The Illusionist's tannins are fine-grained and well-integrated. Most years, the Cabernet Sauvignon is enhanced with small percentages of Cabernet Franc and Petit Verdot depending on the expressions of each varietal for the vintage. Fermentation occurs in large oak tanks and smaller 1.5-ton stainless-steel fermenters before going to barrel. We are focused on letting the grapes shine, without excess interference from either the winemaking team or the oak.

AWARDS AND DISTINCTIONS

93 points – Wine Advocate
95 Points – Wine Spectator,

TECHNICAL DATA

APPELLATION: Columbia Valley
COMPOSITION: Primarily Cabernet Sauvignon with small amounts of Cabernet Franc and Petit Verdot
MATURATION: Aged 20 months in 60% new French oak
CELLARING: Drink over the next 15-20 years

LEARN MORE

Visit our wine store by scanning the image to left

TERTULIA CELLARS WALLA WALLA

Tertulia Cellars operates under the notion that wine is meant to be shared with family and friends, and that warmth is obvious when you visit one of the tasting rooms or vineyards. The word tertulia translates from Latin/Spanish to "social gathering of friends," and the winery emulates this name. With a focus on making wines of quality and distinction from the finest estate vineyards, Tertulia prides itself on creating elegantly approachable wines for the sophisticated palate.

Jim O'Connell began visiting Walla Walla Valley in 2004 and quickly realized the high quality and unique structure of wines from this area. His first vineyard, Whistling Hills, was planted in 2006, then later added Riviere Galets Vineyard in the Rocks District in 2009, and Elevation Vineyard in 2013. Under his direction the winery has produced limited lots of varietals including Cabernet Sauvignon, Syrah, Grenache, Petit Verdot, Viognier, and Marsanne— to name a few. Tertulia Cellars was established in 2005 and now produces an annual average of 3,500 cases. The state-of-the-art winery and cellar were completed in 2008, with a focus on sustainability, functionality, and beauty. Jim also has investments in three Hilton-branded hotels in the state, which gives members of Tertulia Cellars the chance to receive incentives on room rates and other reciprocal benefits.

Tertulia utilizes the most modern winemaking equipment without ignoring Old World techniques and has given the winemaker and viticulture manager— Ryan Raber and Ryan Driver, respectfully—a few key elements that some winemakers only dream of. This includes a Mistral table, which is a high-tech

FACING PAGE: A glimpse of the Vineyard from 1700 feet up. All fractured basalt and above the glacial flood lines. A favorite spot for our vineyard excursions.
Photograph by Richard Duval

ABOVE: Entrance Gate at the winery and Whistling Hills Estate Vineyard in the heart of the southside wineries.
Photograph by Greg Grupenhof

sorting mechanism that does a better job than a team of skilled men, leaving the team with only the best fruit. Interestingly, the machine is named after the strong Mediterranean winds in the Rhone Valley. The team also has their own bottling line. In order to keep the grapes as pure as possible, only three sets of hands ever touch the grapes throughout production: Ryan Driver, Ryan Raber, and the assistant wine maker.

Kristine Bono is Tertulia Cellars' general manager and maintains three tasting rooms located in Walla Walla, Woodinville, and a satellite location in Dundee, Oregon. Her members have come to love a unique feature of the winery: the Petanque club. What exactly is petanque? Think of it as a French version of bocce ball, played with shiny boules in any spot that has suitable dirt and terrain. The membership count includes more than 40 loyal members and continues to grow.

If you visit the Walla Walla tasting room, you'll see the unique petanque terrain next to the estate vineyard.

TOP: The winery utilizes old world techniques to capture the fruit from all three estate vineyards to craft roughly 3,500 cases annually.

BELOW LEFT: The winery is the perfect setting for playing Petanque or just simply sitting and sipping on the patio while enjoying the sunsets.

BELOW RIGHT: A light-filled tasting room with panoramic views of the estate vineyard welcomes guests all year. Experience our wine with our signature pairing plates.
Photographs by Greg Grupenhof

TIERRA LABRADA CABERNET SAUVIGNON

GOURMET PAIRINGS

Pairs well with the classic steak au poivre with frites.

TASTING NOTES

This wine is a concentrated Cabernet Sauvignon with blue-fruit character that is true to the varietal. It has an opulent mid-palate and a wonderfully smooth finish.

WINEMAKER'S INSIGHT

These vines are planted on the Estate Elevation Vineyard along the North Fork of the Walla Walla River, the second highest vineyard in the valley. It's so steep that most of it is terraced, and so rocky that we need a jackhammer to get to the vines. We take the utmost care crafting the wines, using the best French oak and French winemaking techniques.

TECHNICAL DATA

APPELLATION: Walla Walla Valley
COMPOSITION: 90% Cabernet Sauvignon, 7% Merlot, 3% Petit Verdot
MATURATION: 18 months in new French oak
CELLARING: Ages well at 10-15 years

LEARN MORE

Learn more about this wine and our winery by scanning the image on the left

THE GREAT SCHISM

GOURMET PAIRINGS
Lamb shanks braised in red wine.

TASTING NOTES
This wine is a wonderful example of the Southern Rhone-style blends that our Rocks District of Milton-Freewater has produced. It is packed full of raspberry and strawberry fruit preserves, dried fruits, and herbs de Provence. The wine has a wonderful viscosity and mineral notes from the rocky soil, and has a soft and smooth finish.

WINEMAKER'S INSIGHT
Our Riviere Galets vineyard in an ancient dried up riverbed littered with round basalt stones that reach down to 100-300 feet beneath the surface. These stones radiate heat and reflect sunlight making for a round fruit-forward wine with nuances of the soils basalt mineral notes. The wine is aged in large oak vats to avoid an overly oaky finish and emphasizes its high fruit impact.

AWARDS AND DISTINCTIONS
91 points – Wine Enthusiast
94 points – tastings.com

TECHNICAL DATA

APPELLATION: Walla Walla Valley
COMPOSITION: 50% Grenache, 40% Syrah, 7% Cinsault, 3% Mourvèdre
MATURATION: Aged 16 Months in an 800-gallon oak vat.
CELLARING: Ages well at 7-10 years

VISIT OUR STORE

Buy this wine by scanning image on left

The Spanish-style tasting room is warm and contemporary, nestled inside a picturesque location. Outdoor seating is available for picnicking and soaking in the sunshine—with a glass of wine, of course. The Woodinville location is in the Gateway District and is a window-filled space that makes for an ideal spot to relax and gather. Dundee is home to the third location and situated in the heart of the Willamette Valley and premium Pinot Noir country. The tasting room itself lies inside the Inn at Red Hill, a boutique hotel with an attached restaurant, Babica Hen. The experience at this location is driven by a curated seated tasting that educates guests on the premium Bordeaux and Rhone-style wines made by Tertulia Cellars in the Walla Walla Valley.

Tertulia Cellars participates in a variety of public events and festivals, including the Carmenere Festival in November: Paella, Petanque & Rosé in April, Grape to Glass vineyard exploration in August, plus Circle of Friends Cellar dinners year-round.

ABOVE: The "Team of Tertulia" always planning the next exciting thing for this unique program.

BELOW: Sharing his passion for crafting small discreet lots of wine for the sophisticated palate with our guests is the best part of Ryan's day. *Photographs by Richard Duval*

Signature Wines and Wineries of Washington

WALLA WALLA VINTNERS WALLA WALLA

It's not uncommon for people to be passionate about their hobbies, but it's rare that a pair of friends turns a hobby into a thriving company. Yet, Dr. Myles Anderson and Gordy Venneri did just that when they founded Walla Walla Vintners in 1995. As far back as 1981, the friends made small amounts of wine for fun and learned all they could about winemaking, even working alongside some of Walla Walla's pioneering winemakers—including Leonetti's Gary Figgins and Woodward Canyon's Rick Small—before the winery's first release of 675 cases in 1995. Since then, the winery has focused on limited-production, labor-intensive wines including Cabernet Sauvignon, Cabernet Franc, Merlot, Malbec, and Sangiovese that wine critic Paul Gregutt describes as "seductive, soft, and round in the Leonetti mold."

With a humble approach and a commitment to creating the best wine experience possible, the founders of Walla Walla Vintners quickly became known for their collaborative spirit and their belief in creative competition, not adversarial relationships with other winemakers. Dr. Anderson carried that belief in collaboration and giving back to his work at the college level; he helped create the Institute for Enology and Viticulture at Walla Walla Community College to help further the art and science of winemaking in Washington State. He was inducted into the Legends of Washington Wine Hall of Fame in 2011 and received the Lifetime Achievement Award from Washington Association of Wine Grape Growers in 2014. The winery also received the honor of 2016 Pacific Northwest Winery of the Year by Wine Press Northwest. When Dr. Anderson and Gordy Venneri decided it was time to retire—which they did in early 2017—they began envisioning what

FACING PAGE: The magnificent view from above Walla Walla Vintners & their Cut Bank Estate Vineyard featuring the iconic red barn.

ABOVE Owner Scott Haladay showcasing one of the first releases from Walla Walla Vintners Cut Bank Estate Vineyard. *Photographs by Andrea Johnson*

311

CUT BANK ESTATE
CABERNET SAUVIGNON

GOURMET PAIRINGS

Pairs beautifully with blue cheese crusted filet mignon, sautéed morels, and a side of double baked Yukon Gold potatoes.

TASTING NOTES

2012 was the first year of full production of the Estate Vineyard. Aromas of violet, plum, black currant and woody herbs waft out of the glass. Greeted by blackberry on the palate, the Cab opens to flavors of pomegranate, sage and crushed granite all backed by nuanced tannins. The finish is laced with black pepper and dark chocolate covered espresso beans.

WINEMAKER'S INSIGHT

Our Cut Bank Estate Vineyard sits at 1,467 feet in elevation, high for the Walla Walla Valley. Named for the small cliff formed by erosion as Mill Creek flows through the valley, the vineyard is graced by gentle breezes off the Blue Mountains bringing cooler temperatures and just enough precipitation to enable dry-farming. Ideally situated, the southwest exposure provides ample sunshine for slow and even ripening.

TECHNICAL DATA

APPELLATION: Walla Walla Valley
COMPOSITION: 80% Cabernet Sauvignon, 16% Merlot, 4% Petit Verdot
MATURATION: Barrel aged 27 months in 63% new French oak, 11% once-filled French oak and 26% neutral oak barrels.
CELLARING: Approachable upon release, aging beautifully for 15-plus years

LEARN MORE

Buy this wine and more in our store by scanning image on left or visit:
https://www.wallawallavintners.com/Wine

Walla Walla Vintners would look like in the coming years. The founders set their sights on finding someone who knew how to enhance established companies to help them grow, as well as someone who shared their passion for wine. That person was Scott Haladay, who became an owner-partner in February 2017 and brought with him a 20-year career in technology, sales, and marketing, including 10 years developing software for beverage distributors.

With an eye to the future, Walla Walla Vintners maintains its dedication to Old-World winemaking techniques under the direction of their longtime winemaker, William vonMetzger. In 2017, he oversaw the inaugural release of the Cut Bank Estate Vineyard Cabernet Sauvignon and Vottavo, Walla Walla Vintners' prized Super Tuscan-inspired blend, the latest additions to the winery's legacy.

TOP: The winemaker and owner welcome you to join them in the newly remodeled tasting room through our iconic barn doors.

BELOW Owner & winemaker sampling newly released estate wines under the shade trees of the pastoral picnic area while also soaking up the beautiful views.
Photographs by Andrea Johnson

WATERBROOK WINERY WALLA WALLA

Established in 1984, Waterbrook Winery is a Walla Walla, Washington, pioneer, producing wines that exemplify Northwest modern style and the outstanding vineyards from which they are sourced. Today, Waterbrook features a state-of-the-art winery, a robust tasting room hospitality program, and a 49-acre estate vineyard in the Walla Walla Valley AVA.

Whether sourcing from the Walla Walla Valley or the greater Columbia Valley, every detail of Waterbrook's production is carried out by a committed team led by winemaker John Freeman. With more than 80 90-plus scores and 100 Best Buy wines, John masterfully approaches the unique qualities of each vineyard and vintage to produce wines that are true to variety, full of depth and structure, and representative of Columbia Valley's best.

Visitors to the Waterbrook tasting room may relax on the patio with a glass of their favorite wine while enjoying the tranquil surroundings. Waterbrook also boasts a full-service menu of farm-to-table fare, utilizing local and seasonal ingredients designed to pair with the award-winning wines.

FACING PAGE The beautiful grounds of the Waterbrook Tasting Room located in Walla Walla..

ABOVELEFT: Winemaker John Freeman standing in front of the Waterbrook Winery.

ABOVE RIGHT: A delicious selection of food and wine pairings from the full-service menu available at the Waterbrook tasting room.
Photographs by Josiah Michael

INDEX

Callan Cellars 29
18742 142nd Avenue NE
Woodinville, WA 98072
425.829.5448
www.callancellars.com
Hours: Sat, 12 – 5pm,
or by appointment

Canoe Ridge Vineyard 245
1102 West Cherry Street
Walla Walla, WA 99362
509.525.1843
www.canoeridgevineyard.com
Open daily 11am – 4pm

Cascade Cliffs Vineyard & Winery 135
8866 Highway 14
Wishram, WA 98673
509.767.1100

Hood River Tasting Room
211 Oak Street
Hood River, OR 97031
541.436.4215

Woodinville Tasting Room
15029 Woodinville-Redmond
Road NE #300
Woodinville, WA 98072
425.398.9520

Cave B Estate Winery 141
Quincy Tasting Room
348 Silica Road NW
Quincy, WA 98848
509.785.3500
www.caveb.com

Woodinville Tasting Room
14356 Woodinville-Redmond Road
Redmond, WA 98052
425.949.7152
Open to public, hours are seasonal

Chateau Ste. Michelle 31
14111 NE 145th Street
Woodinville, WA 98072
425.488.1133
www.ste-michelle.com
Open daily 10am – 5pm

College Cellars of Walla Walla 247
3020 Isaacs Avenue
Walla Walla, WA 99362
www.Collegecellars.com
509.524.5170
Hours: Thur – Sun, 11am – 5pm

Columbia Crest Winery 147
178810 State Rt. 221
Paterson, WA 99345
509.875.4227
www.columbiacrest.com
Open daily 10am – 5pm

Columbia Winery 35
14030 NE 145th Street
Woodinville, WA 98072
425.482.7490
www.columbiawinery.com
Hours: Sat – Thur, 11am – 6pm
Fridays 11am – 7pm

Damsel Cellars 41
18744 142nd Avenue NE
Woodinville, WA 98072
206.465.2433
www.damselcellars.com
Hours: Sat, 1pm – 5pm
and by appointment

DeLille Cellars 45
Carriage House Tasting Room
14421 Woodinville-Redmond Road N.E.
Woodinville, WA 98072
www.delillecellars.com
425.877.9472
Open daily

Maison DeLille Wine Lounge
15 Lake Street
Kirkland, WA 98033
www.maisondelille.com
425.489.0544
Hours vary seasonally

Den Hoed Wine Estates 149
3861 1st Avenue South #B
Seattle, Washington 98134
509.882.4233
Hours: Fridays, 3pm – 6pm
Saturdays, 12 – 6pm

Doubleback Winery 249
3853 Powerline Road
Walla Walla, WA 99362
509.525.3334
www.doubleback.com
Open by appointment only

Dunham Cellars 255
150 East Boeing Avenue
Walla Walla, WA 99362
509.529.4685
www.dunhamcellars.com
Open daily 11am – 4pm

Eternal Wines 261
9 South 1st Avenue or 602 Piper Avenue
Walla Walla, WA 99362
509.240.6258
www.Eternalwine.com

Fielding Hills Winery 155
565 South Lakeshore Rd
Chelan, WA 98816
509.888.WINE (9463)
www.Fieldinghills.com
Hours: Seasonally, 11 – 5 pm
Custom tours available

Five Star Cellars 263
840 C Street
Walla Walla, WA 99362
509.527.8400
www.fivestarcellars.com
Hours: Saturday, 10am – 4pm,
or by appointment

Foundry Vineyards 265
1111 Abadie St.
Walla Walla, WA 99362
509.529.0736
www.foundryvineyards.com
Hours: Thur – Sun, 11am – 5pm
Mon – Wed, by appointment

Hamilton Cellars 161
55410 North Sunset Road
Benton City, WA 99320
509.628.8227
www.hamiltoncellars.com
Hours: Sun – Thurs ,11am – 5pm
Fri & Sat 11am – 6pm

Hedges Family Estate 165
53511 N. Sunset Road
Benton City, WA 99320
509.588.3155
www.hedgesfamilyestate.com
For tasting hours call the winery
or visit our website

Henry Earl Estate Wines 269
25 East Main Street
Walla Walla, WA 99362
www.henryearlwines.com
509.876.2459
Hours: Mon – Thurs 12 – 6pm
Fri – Sat, 12 – 8pm,
Sun 11 am – 5pm

J. Bookwalter Winery 173
894 Tulip Lane
Richland, WA 99352
509.627.5000
www.bookwalterwines.com
Open daily, 12 – 5pm

Woodinville Tasting Studio
14810 NE 145th Street
Building B
Woodinville, WA 98072
425.488.1983
Sun – Fri, 12 – 6 pm
Saturday, 12 – 7pm

Kasia Winery 47
905 First Street
Snohomish, WA 98290
900 Front Street
Leavenworth, WA 98826
425.941.0224
www.kasiawinery.com

INDEX

Photographs by Richard Duval

Other titles that might interest you...

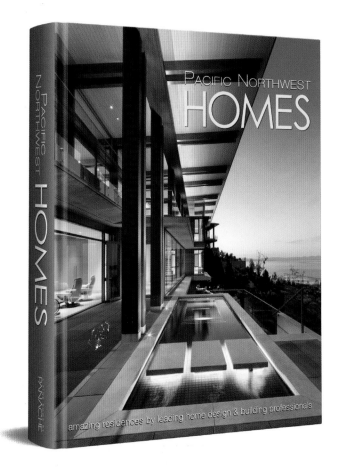

On Sale Now!

PACIFIC NORTHWEST HOMES

Amazing residences by leading home design and building professionals

Explore the best of metropolitan and waterfront living in a stunning collection of beautiful homes by the Pacific Northwest's top airchitects, interior designers, and custom building professionals. Including those who have become icons in their industry, as well as those who are quickly making a name for themselves, Pacific Northwest Homes offers a glimpse into the thoughtful processes and philosophies behind the region's most distinctive homes. Vivid photographs, personal quotes, and graceful captions facilitate your journey as you meet the brilliant artisans, architects, designers, and builders who transform everyday materials into homes that speak to the soul.

From nature-inspired country elegance to modem urban living, and everything in between, this magnificent 400-page collection includes something for every taste and every budget. Whether jumping into a new construction project, remodeling an existing dwelling, or simply looking for inspiration, Pacific Northwest Homes is sure to impress and inspire.

scan image above to preview book

SIGNATURE WINES & WINERIES
of Coastal California

Explore the rolling hills of bucolic vineyards and funky, offbeat urban wineries in a stunning collection of the best wineries and finest wines from the best wine professionals along California's coast—from Monterey County, to Paso Robles and San Luis Obispo, to Santa Ynez Valley and Santa Barbara. Including the pioneer winemakers who have become icons in the wine industry, as well as those who are quickly making a name for themselves, *Signature Wines & Wineries of Coastal California* offers a comprehensive view into the meticulous winemaking processes and philosophies behind the region's most distinctive wines. Vivid photographs, personal stories, and graceful captions facilitate your journey as you meet the brilliant winemakers and winery owners who cultivate exquisite wines from bud to bottle. Each wine featured within includes meticulous tasting notes and winemakers' insights as well as gourmet food pairings to help you plan your next dinner party. As anyone who as has been to California's coastal wine country will attest, no one is a stranger for long. Sit back with your favorite glass of wine, and savor the beauty and splendor of this exclusive collection that captures the art of winemaking, the richness of the land, regional architecture, and history of each vineyard, as well as anecdotes of the people behind current and future favorite labels. *Signature Wines & Wineries of Washington* is sure to delight your senses.

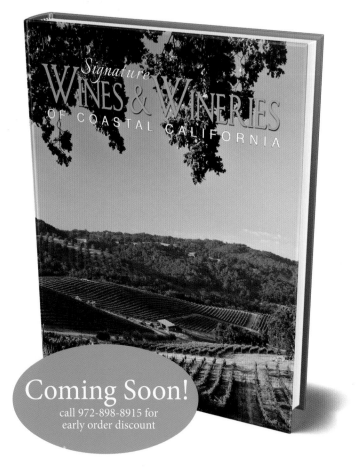

Coming Soon!
call 972-898-8915 for
early order discount

preview book

Available through all major book stores and Amazon.com
or call Intermedia Publishing at 972-898-8915 for quantity discounts

Photograph by Kathryn Elsesser for Long Shadows Vintners, page 277